Occasionally I hear someone on television talking about how they are afraid of flying or how they can't get over their trauma, and I find myself thinking, Why don't they just read Fred Gallo's book *Energy Tapping for Trauma* and get over it? Gallo has written an easy-to-read, accessible book that anyone can use to move on from fear, phobias, trauma, and pain, as well as just giving themselves an emotional or energy tune-up. Read it, and tap into your inner healer.

—Bill O'Hanlon, author of *Change 101*

ENERGY TAPPING

for

TRAUMA

Rapid Relief from
Post-Traumatic Stress
Using Energy Psychology

FRED P. GALLO, PH.D.

New Harbinger Publications, Inc.

Publisher's Note

This publication is designed to provide accurate and authoritative information in regard to the subject matter covered. It is sold with the understanding that the publisher is not engaged in rendering psychological, financial, legal, or other professional services. If expert assistance or counseling is needed, the services of a competent professional should be sought.

Advanced Energy Psychology (AEP), Alpha-Theta Breathing, Container Technique, Eight-Step Process (ESP), Energy Consciousness Therapy (ECT), Energy Diagnostic and Treatment Methods (EDxTM), Energy Tapping (ET), Healing Energy Light Process (HELP), Midline Energy Treatment (MET), Negative Affect Erasing Method (NAEM), Trauma Removal Technique (TRT), and Unified Self Process (USP) are trademarked terms and techniques by Fred P. Gallo, PhD.

Distributed in Canada by Raincoast Books

Copyright © 2007 by Fred P. Gallo
New Harbinger Publications, Inc.
5674 Shattuck Avenue
Oakland, CA 94609
www.newharbinger.com

Acquired by Jess O'Brien; Cover design by Amy Shoup;
Edited by Jean Blomquist; Text design by Tracy Carlson

Library of Congress Cataloging-in-Publication Data

Gallo, Fred P.
  Energy tapping for trauma : rapid relief from post-traumatic stress using energy psychology / Fred P. Gallo.
     p. cm.
  Includes bibliographical references.
  ISBN-13: 978-1-57224-501-3
  ISBN-10: 1-57224-501-8
  1. Energy psychology. 2. Post-traumatic stress disorder--Alternative treatment. I. Title.
RC489.E53G3553 2007
616.89--dc22

                    2007018497

09 08 07

10 9 8 7 6 5 4 3 2 1

First printing

To Hanna, Aidan, Michael, Ryan, and all future grandchildren

To the memory of Hugo, who blessed us with his love

Contents

Foreword

Have you ever found yourself caught up in a pattern of behavior that doesn't support you or the outcome you desire? What stops you from doing what you know you should do? Do you ever wish that there was a simple solution that could interrupt this pattern—right as it was happening—a solution that would allow your true intentions to shine through?

You are now holding in your hands a guide to one of the most powerful methods I know for rapidly overcoming stress, obstacles, and even trauma that may have held you back from living your life filled with passion, love, and accomplishment. Over the past thirty years, I've had the privilege of working with literally millions of people who come from widely diverse backgrounds and beliefs. What I've observed over and over again is that 80 percent of success in life is psychology and 20 percent is mechanics. Most people know what to do—but they don't do what they know.

Although we're all unique, I've found there is one common emotion that stops many people from living to their utmost potential. You can call this emotion by many names: mistrust, guilt, embarrassment, doubt, even anger—but, ultimately, the emotion underlying all others is *fear*. And if this fear is big enough to hold you back from doing what you know you should do, I believe it is the result of a belief system that is so strong it has actually created an energy blockage in your body.

One subtle but powerful way to change your physiology is to understand the patterns of energy within your body and learn how to send a vibration into your body that breaks a pattern using just a simple tapping motion. And you can use this simple technique whether you're trying to simply interrupt your current pattern of frustration or stress, stop yourself from crying or falling apart in the moment, or to overcome the impact of a profound trauma.

You may think that this is just another "New Age, polish up your aura, vibrate with more joy" type of technique. However, this is a proven science, as detailed in a groundbreaking study by physician and acupuncturist Dr. Joaquin Andrade. The study, which involved 5,000 participants, demonstrated that patients with post-traumatic stress disorder (and many other conditions) who were treated with tapping experienced better results more rapidly than patients who were treated with more traditional methods. The difference was in the dramatic results—76 percent of the patients who experienced tapping were completely cured, as opposed to only 51 percent of those who were treated with traditional techniques. This study proves that tapping is an extremely effective, efficient tool, and I wouldn't be recommending it to you unless I knew it from my own experience—and by its science.

So much of what I've learned about the powerful role that energy plays in the body has been through the work of Fred Gallo—a man who has dedicated his life to helping people discover how to clear the blockages that hold them back. In *Energy Tapping for Trauma,* Fred Gallo presents easy-to-master tools to help you jolt your body, break the pattern, and completely shift your energy and emotions in the moment.

Energy tapping is derived from a field of study called Energy Psychology. The foundation of Energy Psychology is built on two principal findings: (1) When you have a psychological problem, there is a disruption in your body's energy system. (2) Techniques that return your body's energy system to balance will eliminate the problem.

I passionately believe that all change is created in a moment. Emotion is created by motion—in other words, your body leads your emotions. Even the most minute changes in our facial expressions or our gestures will shift the way that we're feeling in any moment, and, therefore, the way we evaluate our lives—the way we think and the way we act.

The concept of energy tapping engages the power of shifting your physiology in order to shift your emotional state. It is a powerful tool to eliminate traumatic events and emotional patterns that have become stuck in your body. It assists in breaking those patterns and releasing them. I, personally, have witnessed people who have undergone years of traditional therapy break through emotional blockages in just a matter of moments by using the principles of energy tapping presented in this book.

For human beings to experience lasting fulfillment, we must live a life that is aligned with our true purpose—that which brings us most in harmony with fulfilling our ultimate potential in life. If you could find a way to rapidly eliminate painful emotions so that you could live your potential to your fullest, would you try it?

If your answer is a resounding yes, then I strongly encourage you to master the techniques discussed in this book. It won't take long, and it will change your life.

—With love and respect,
Anthony Robbins

Acknowledgments

Newton emphasized, "If I have seen further than others, it is by standing upon the shoulders of giants." Similarly, if what I have written has more to offer those who suffer from trauma, it is because it rests on heritage. Therefore I would like to acknowledge all who contributed to this work, even those whom I have not personally met.

I am grateful to those who discovered our body's energy system as an access to health and happiness. I am also grateful to George J. Goodheart, John Thie, John Diamond, Roger Callahan, and others who have pioneered the use of this system in the mission of helping others.

I would also like to thank my wife, family, friends, and colleagues for their support and encouragement throughout the writing of this book. I would also like to thank David and Justin Lee for their assistance with the illustrations used in *Energy Tapping for Trauma*.

Finally, thank you to all the talented people at New Harbinger Publications, including Matt McKay, publisher, and Jess O'Brien, acquisitions editor. Special appreciation and acknowledgment go to Heather Mitchener, editorial director, and Jean M. Blomquist, copyeditor, for their energetic attention throughout the writing of this book.

Introduction

We can't solve problems by using the same kind of thinking we used when we created them.

—Albert Einstein

Welcome to *Energy Tapping for Trauma*! You're about to embark on an exciting adventure of discovering some of the most unique, useful, and hope-inspiring healing concepts and techniques available. But perhaps you're just leafing through these pages and trying to decide if you should buy this book. Or possibly you bought it already and you're wondering if it's really worth reading. Maybe you just liked the cover or the illustrations. Or possibly you just borrowed it from a friend. Regardless, reading and applying the techniques in this book will prove well worth your time and effort. I hope you'll find this to be an investment that will pay handsome dividends for life.

Why Read This Book?

Probably you've already read, viewed, and/or listened to other self-help books or audio-visual materials on overcoming trauma. Some of them were excellent, some were okay, and some were ... well ... just so-so. And all this has been part of your search and commitment to find solutions to the problems that led you to this book. But this is a very different kind of self-help and help-others book. Through it, we will be partners, working together so that you'll ultimately get the help you need and the results you want. I cover many techniques here that are not contained in my other publications. Primarily this is a self-help book, although it is also intended as a resource for therapists and their clients. Because self-help books are not and cannot be a substitute for counseling, psychotherapy, or other forms of medical treatment, I want to emphasize the following: This book is not intended to diagnose or treat any psychological or medical condition. However, many people are able to use what's covered here to get results they never dreamed possible. But if your issues are so upsetting and debilitating that these techniques do not work for you, there is abundant hope. Often working with a healthy, competent, caring therapist who is knowledgeable about *energy psychology* (EP) and *energy tapping* (ET) is just what's needed. These terms describe the technique of exerting energy (such as by physically tapping) to treat a problem, and they also recognize that everything is made of energy, even our thoughts and emotions. Sometimes it's not enough to apply these techniques on your own. And that's where a knowledgeable therapist or coach is invaluable. If you are already working with a therapist, this book can be used to supplement your therapy. Let your therapist know about this so that you can work together with these concepts and techniques (as well as others that your therapist finds important) for your benefit. If you do not have a therapist trained in this approach, you may be able to locate a professional in your area by visiting www.energypsych.com or writing to me at fgallo@energypsych.com.

The ideas and techniques covered here are really different and could literally blow your mind! Well, maybe not your whole mind—just those things in your mind that have been giving you a hard time. That's what happened when I started studying, practicing, and developing this approach nearly thirty years ago. In many respects, my search began about forty-eight years ago, since I've been on a nearly lifelong mission of discovering and developing ways to help myself and others. These techniques have been used by thousands of people with satisfying results. And you'll reap the same kind of rewards.

Also, in my enthusiasm, dedication, and obsession, I've written seven books and many book chapters, articles, and manuals on this approach. And, with the mission of helping professionals to better help themselves, their patients, and their clients, I've traveled widely to teach these ideas and techniques to thousands worldwide. So you see, I'm really dug-in and committed to making a contribution, and I know that what I'm about to reveal to you really works. I think you've gathered that by now. There is also mounting research that attests to the validity of these statements, but ultimately you will be the judge of that.

Simple Yet Powerful Techniques

Here we cover simple yet powerful techniques and commonsense principles that you can use to rapidly and thoroughly eliminate the emotional distress of trauma, including nightmares, intrusive thoughts, flashbacks, anxiety, startle response, depression, and many associated physical symptoms. This book will help nearly anyone who experiences distress caused by overwhelming and catastrophic events, including hurricanes, tornados, earthquakes, war, rape, accidents, personal injury, disabilities, loss of a loved one, and more. And the information can also be used to rapidly eliminate other painful emotions associated with rejection, insult, embarrassment, shame, and more. Basically this book offers you knowledge and simple techniques to eliminate traumatic stress and to get on with a happier and healthier life.

To some extent, *Energy Tapping for Trauma* is a sequel to *Energy Tapping* (Gallo and Vincenzi 2000), a popular book that my good friend Dr. Harry Vincenzi and I published several years ago. *Energy Tapping* introduced some of the techniques covered here, although that book has a much broader focus and does not exclusively deal with the effects of traumatic and other painful memories. This book specifically focuses on how to reduce and remove traumatic stress and covers many additional techniques developed since the publication of *Energy Tapping*. It also includes others that could only be learned by attending seminars and studying professional publications. In many ways, this book is simpler than many previous books on trauma, and it stands as a significant advancement in energy psychology (Gallo 2005). However, since *Energy Tapping* contains information and techniques for dealing with emotional issues other than trauma, applying the information from both books is highly recommended.

What's Different About This Approach?

How can you expect to benefit from this book? What can you expect to learn that's different from other books on trauma? You know, there are lots of books out there about getting over trauma and some are quite good. Some discuss the causes and symptoms of trauma, and that kind of information is covered here as well. Others offer cognitive strategies for overcoming trauma—you know, challenge and change your thinking—and in a very different and unique way you get that here too. Still other books teach behavioral techniques, such as changing your behavior and your environment, and that's also uniquely covered in this book. And still others offer visualization techniques to self-soothe and project a positive future. We've got that here too, with techniques like the Healing Energy Light Process (HELP)™, which combines visualization with a number of other innovative features. So that touches on the similarities and hints at some differences, but what's really different about this book? And why should you spend your valuable time reading it? Good questions! And the answer is simple.

Rapidly Eliminate Trauma

Energy Tapping for Trauma will show you how to quickly and easily eliminate traumatic and other painful memories and emotions on your own. Frequently all you have to do is briefly think about the upsetting event, rate the level of emotional discomfort on a 0 to 10 scale (often called subjective units of discomfort, subjective units of distress, or simply SUD), and then apply some very simple techniques. Many of the techniques involve tapping lightly with a couple fingertips at key locations on your body, breathing in very specific ways, holding certain body postures and gestures, and doing some other activities that may seem a bit unusual. And while the memory of the painful event is usually not erased, these techniques almost always eliminate the distressing emotions of the event within a matter of a few minutes and sometimes in just a few seconds. And, as a rule, the relief lasts permanently. Actually, in some instances the memory might be even more vivid and maybe you'll have some insights about it that were previously elusive, but the emotional upset will be gone.

Sounds too simple to be true, doesn't it? Well as hard as it is to believe, it's easy and it works. And it doesn't matter if the incident happened a long time ago or just the other day. There are a few things to take into account to make sure that the process gets you the results you want, but as your personal coach and partner, I'll show you what to do. And before you know it, you won't be bothered by memories of unpleasant or awful events. That means you won't get upset or get startled easily, or have nightmares or feel depressed, or be tormented by awful memories. When you think about the event, it will be absolutely and completely in the past, just like any other memory that has no emotional charge connected to it. In other words, the problem—the trauma—will be gone for good! And as a result of this significant shift, which usually occurs quickly, your feelings and your quality of life will change for the better.

How and Why It Works

But what are the tapping and other physical techniques about anyway? Although it sounds odd, it isn't really all that odd, since frequently you do many similar things. When you're feeling tired, you yawn and stretch to try to relieve yourself of fatigue.

You don't think about this much, but sometimes after you yawn and stretch a few times, you feel better. If you have a headache or neck pain, you hold or exert pressure on your head or rub your neck, and this may give you some level of relief too. If you get a cramp in your leg, you might hold it and squeeze it tightly; this often relieves the cramping. Or if a friend chokes on some food, you might perform a simple physical technique—the Heimlich maneuver—and dislodge the food from his or her windpipe instantly. If someone suffered cardiac arrest, you might perform cardiopulmonary resuscitation (CPR) and save the person's life. Well, you might think of these energy-tapping trauma techniques as the psychological and emotional equivalent of CPR or the Heimlich maneuver.

As I mentioned above, I refer to these techniques as energy tapping (ET) and the overall approach as energy psychology (EP). Energy psychology recognizes that everything is made of energy, even our thoughts and emotions. You can think of energy in very practical and scientific terms, although, in some respects, energy also seems to have a mystical quality. Everything is made of energy: the stars, the planets, asteroids, the air we breathe, our bodies, our brains, the cars we drive. According to Albert Einstein, all matter is basically energy in a relatively stable form. That is what $E=mc^2$ means: matter and energy are equivalent. By energy tapping, we exert energy to treat a concrete problem.

When you have a psychological problem, there are many things going on. Let's take trauma, for example, since that is the focus of this book. When you have a trauma, you hold a memory of the traumatic event, something awful that happened. But it's more than that. You also attach negative emotions, such as anxiety, anger, guilt, and possibly panic, to the memory. The memory, which involves internal images, sounds, smells, and so on, triggers emotional and physical reactions. This is an energetic event, similar to electricity traveling through a wire after a switch has been turned on. You can think of these techniques as ways to turn off that switch and thereby remove the emotional part of the memory. As a result, any thoughts about the traumatic event become emotionally neutral (or nearly so) even when you are not consciously thinking about the event. That's why the nightmares, flashbacks, depression, and other negative emotions and sensations stop. At its most basic, the underlying cause of the problem is treated with ET.

There are many ways to explain the principle involved with these techniques. But essentially what we've discovered is that stimulating the body in specific ways (e.g., tapping at key locations on the body, such as acupoints) while bringing to mind a disturbing memory changes the emotional reaction to the memory in the brain and body as a whole. Basically these procedures change the structure and the meaning of the experience, similar to the way the word "go" can be changed by adding the letters "o" and "d" to create the word "good," or the letters in "dog" can be rearranged to create the word "God." Obviously, the words "go," "good," "dog," and "God" have different meanings and they give you different feelings. Similarly, the emotional-physical aspects of a memory have a different structure after tapping has been added to the mix.

Another way to think of this is to liken the emotional memory to the electromagnetic patterns on an audiotape or videotape that produce specific sounds and/or images when it is played. That's essentially what the audiotape and videotape data are, just static electricity that can be erased by exposing the tape to a strong electromagnetic field. Memories in our brains and bodies have a similar yet more complex structure. Nonetheless, the negative emotions associated with a memory are electrical and chemical processes that can be changed—often as easily as they were formed in the first place.

Now that might sound somewhat complicated, but there are many ways to explain why energy-tapping techniques work. We'll discuss this in more detail later and hopefully it will make more sense. But just as you don't have to know how to build or repair a car or a computer in order to use them, it is not necessary to understand the theoretical basis of why ET works in order for you to successfully use it to feel better. All you have to do is use it!

How to Read This Book

Although you will understand the basis of the method and how to apply it best if you read this entire book, you may know that most books are bought and not read. They remain prominently displayed on bookshelves like trophies or stored in boxes; perhaps their owners only read a few pages, if any. Since you've already read this far, it's likely that you are not in the trophy or box category. However, I want you to benefit as much as possible from this book. So while reading the entire book is recommended, I recognize that your time is valuable and that there's much more to your life than this book. To save you some time, here's a brief outline of the chapters so that you can make an informed choice about what to read.

Chapter 1 (What Is Trauma?) discusses the differences among traumatic events, traumatic memories, trauma, and post-traumatic stress disorder (PTSD). A brief checklist is provided to help you determine if you or a loved one suffers from PTSD. Other conditions resulting from trauma, such as adjustment disorders, phobias, and panic, are also briefly discussed. I distinguish obvious trauma from more subtle forms and introduce some theory. A couple of traumatic instances from my own life are covered in some detail, along with how these traumas were resolved, especially through energy psychology.

In chapter 2 (Customary Treatments for Trauma), traditional treatments for trauma resolution are briefly covered. These include medication, "flooding" or emotional reliving, group therapy, family therapy, and cognitive behavioral therapy. I thought you might like to know something about what many consider to be "standard of care" (the therapeutic approaches that are generally used for trauma) before covering some newer approaches that often afford swifter results. Many therapists who apply customary approaches are increasingly integrating their work with ET.

Chapter 3 (Complementary and Alternative Treatments for Trauma) provides you with a basic overview of some alternative and promising ways of treating trauma, including visual-kinesthetic dissociation (V/KD), eye movement desensitization and reprocessing (EMDR), traumatic incident reduction (TIR), and thought field therapy (TFT). These techniques are outlined briefly along with some case examples and discussion of what accounts for their effectiveness.

Chapter 4 (The New Energy Psychology) provides an overview of energy psychology and discusses the history, theory, and major techniques included in this approach. Case examples are presented. In this chapter, you will also explore some of the scientific aspects of energy psychology and energy tapping.

Chapter 5 (How to Use Energy Tapping for Trauma) provides specific and detailed instruction and guidelines on how to apply several highly effective and efficient energy psychology techniques to eliminate trauma. These techniques include emotional stress release (ESR), frontal/occipital holding (FOH), Alpha-Theta Breathing™, energy tapping for simple trauma, energy tapping for highly complex trauma, Midline Energy Treatment (MET)™, Trauma Removal Technique (TRT)™, and the Eight-Step Process (ESP)™. We begin with the simplest and work our way up to relatively more complex. However, all of these techniques are quite easy to learn and apply.

Chapter 6 (Troubleshooting) is an important chapter to use when the techniques covered in chapter 5 are not giving you the results you would like. This chapter covers various troubleshooting adjustments and also includes ways to prevent severe emotional reactions from occurring during self-treatment.

Chapter 7 (Reconnecting to and Empowering Your Life) covers positive reprogramming and how to reconnect to your life in positive ways after a trauma has been removed. Positive reprogramming involves working with your thoughts. At some level, trauma is maintained in your thoughts. When you realize deeply that you are the thinker, you can dismiss trauma thoughts and memories as they occur. This is accomplished by learning how to observe the thought or memory, seeing it as thought, and then not becoming attached to it as something that is real. Reconnecting to your life in positive ways includes methods of accessing and instilling gratitude and compassion, focusing on your best possible self (BPS), building a firm sense of helpful resources, and using these resources to resolve past issues. The Healing Energy Light Process (HELP) is also covered in detail.

Chapter 8 (Beginnings) briefly summarizes what has been covered, explores more deeply why these techniques work, and provides some final considerations on how to apply these methods to enhance your life.

Appendix A (Acronyms) lists acronyms for acupoints, tapping techniques, and other terms used frequently in this book.

Appendix B (Research in Energy Psychology) goes into detail about research that has been conducted in the area of energy psychology.

Appendix C (Resources) covers various resources that will enable you both to explore energy psychology and energy tapping in more depth and to locate a qualified therapist.

That gives you some idea about what's covered in the following chapters. Thank you for picking up this book. As you read about and absorb information on trauma and the techniques that can free you from the pain of trauma you have experienced, I hope you will enjoy the journey and benefit greatly from it. My best wishes to you.

1

What Is Trauma?

Life means suffering.
The origin of suffering is attachment.
The cessation of suffering is attainable.

—Siddhártha Gautama

Although trauma also refers to physical injury, this chapter is about the psychological trauma that occurs after a traumatic event. Psychological trauma can be caused by physical injury, abuse, crime, violence, rape, war, extreme poverty, and more. All of these events involve feelings of helplessness in the face of a real or imagined threat to your life, bodily integrity, or mental health, and they overpower your ability to cope with the memories and emotions involved. Traumatic events frequently result in extreme states of insecurity and confusion, and challenge your model of the world. However, not everyone reacts to similar events in the same way. One person may experience the event as traumatic while another may not. Not everyone who experiences a traumatic event will develop psychological trauma or post-traumatic stress disorder (PTSD). But if you are left with trauma, this book can show you ways to eliminate it.

Post-Traumatic Stress Disorder (PTSD)

Post-traumatic stress disorder (PTSD) is a chronic and devastating psychological problem that often occurs after traumatic events such as rape, assault, mugging, terrorism, and war. About 30 percent of Vietnam veterans developed PTSD at some point after the war (Kulka et al. 1988) and similar statistics can be expected from the war in Iraq. Prior to more enlightened times, soldiers in military battle who developed this condition were first diagnosed with shell shock and later with combat neurosis. Unfortunately many were mistakenly considered malingerers and were sent back to the front lines to suffer with their impaired conditions.

PTSD includes symptoms such as flashbacks (vividly reexperiencing the traumatic event), hallucinations (seeing, hearing, or feeling things that are not real), nightmares, intrusive thoughts, sleep problems, difficulty concentrating, depression, emotional numbing, pervasive anxiety, panic attacks, and more. It is estimated that 70 percent of adults in the United States will experience one or more traumatic events in their lives, and 20 percent or more will go on to develop PTSD. Approximately 3.5 percent of Americans age eighteen and older—more than 7.7 million people—suffer from PTSD at any given time (Kessler et al. 2005). That's a lot of people and massive amounts of suffering from trauma! And we're only talking about America. PTSD is even more prevalent in war-torn areas of the world, such as Gaza where the rate is 18 percent or Algeria where the incidence is as high as 37 percent. About 80 percent of people with PTSD developed the disorder after being raped, severely beaten, physically assaulted, or exposed to war; 20 percent are accounted for by vehicular accidents and other kinds of traumatic events (de Jong et al. 2001). While people contend with other terrible things in life, trauma and PTSD alone amount to much suffering and cause a significant drain on human resources.

Traumatic Stress

Traumatic events and resulting traumatic stress (also referred to as trauma) can lead to many types of psychological problems. In addition to PTSD, the most commonly diagnosed condition is acute stress disorder (ASD), which refers to traumatic stress that lasts no longer than four weeks. After that period, PTSD is used to describe serious symptoms resulting from traumatic events. Both disorders assume that the person experienced an event that involved actual or threatened injury or death to themselves or others, and that they felt fear, helplessness, or horror at the time.

Traumatic stress symptoms are categorized as "intrusions," which means reexperiencing the event in nightmares and flashbacks (episodes in which the traumatic event is vividly revisited); "avoidance," which involves shying away from people, places, and things that can trigger the intrusive memories; and "hyperarousal," which involves physical reactions, such as perpetually being on edge (hypervigilance) and exaggerated startle response or jumpiness in response to a touch, an unexpected motion, or a loud noise. To some extent these symptoms have survival value, since they motivate the trauma victim to be on alert for similarly dangerous situations. But when a person who is no longer in danger continues to operate in survival mode, the responses that once provided protection now endanger physical and psychological health. Chronic traumatic stress impairs emotional and social functioning, and can lead to health complications such as chronic muscle tension and pain, ulcers, and susceptibility to infections.

Not everyone exposed to a traumatic event develops ASD or PTSD, and many people who develop traumatic stress resolve it on their own without the need for therapy. Resilience seems to be the result of a number of factors, including developmental history, personal resources, perceptions about and meaning given to the event, and environmental support. However, sometimes PTSD develops long after the traumatic event occurred, even years later. And there are many other psychological or physical conditions, such as adjustment disorders, phobias, generalized anxiety, and fibromyalgia, that can develop after traumatic episodes. So it often makes good sense to consult a mental health professional with expertise in traumatology (the study and treatment of trauma) if you suffer a severe traumatic incident. The techniques and concepts covered in this book are highly effective in treating trauma and also may be helpful in preventing the development of PTSD or other serious psychological problems.

Do You Have PTSD?

Although only a qualified mental health professional can diagnose PTSD, here is a checklist, adapted from the fourth edition of the *Diagnostic and Statistical Manual of Mental Disorders* (American Psychiatric Association 2000), that can help to determine if you have symptoms of traumatic stress or PTSD. (Symptoms may vary in young children.)

PTSD CHECKLIST FOR ADULTS

- ☐ You experienced, witnessed, or were confronted with an event(s) involving actual or threatened death or serious injury, or a threat to your or someone else's physical integrity and your reaction involved extreme fear, helplessness, or shock.

- ☐ You persistently relive the event in one or more of the following ways:
    - ☐ Frequent distressing thoughts, images, or perceptions of the event
    - ☐ Frequent distressing dreams of the event
    - ☐ Acting or feeling as though the events were returning (reliving it)
    - ☐ Intense upset to thoughts or situations that resemble aspects of the event
    - ☐ Physical reactions to thoughts or situations that resemble aspects of the event

- ☐ You frequently experience three or more of the following:
    - ☐ Avoid thoughts, feelings, or conversations about the event
    - ☐ Avoid people, places, or activities that arouse recall of the event
    - ☐ Inability to remember significant aspects of the event
    - ☐ Significantly lower interest or involvement in important activities
    - ☐ Feeling disconnected or distant from other people
    - ☐ Limited range of feelings (e.g., loss of pleasurable feelings)
    - ☐ Feeling that your future is shortened or impaired

- ☐ You frequently experience two or more of the following:
    - ☐ Sleep problems
    - ☐ Irritability or anger episodes
    - ☐ Concentration problems
    - ☐ Exaggerated attention to possible danger (hypervigilance)
    - ☐ Exaggerated startle response

- ☐ This disturbance causes you major suffering or impairment in important areas of your life (e.g., social, job, school, etc.).

Adopted with permission from the *Diagnostic and Statistical Manual of Mental Disorders*, 4th edition, text revision, copyright 2000. American Psychiatric Association.

Other Disorders of Trauma

We've already focused on the obvious traumatic events that frequently result in PTSD, but "lesser" distressing events can also be highly traumatic. A child having a tooth extraction, undergoing surgery, or being severely punished can suffer long-lasting trauma. Being rejected by a friend or lover can cause traumatic stress, even if the reaction does not qualify as PTSD. Since trauma always involves your perception of the event, a seemingly minor incident can result in traumatic stress, while an obviously awful event may not have lasting impact at all.

Most psychological problems and many physical problems can be traced back to psychosocial stressors, which involve traumatic events in one form or another. Phobias, depression, panic disorders, many personality disorders, multiple personality disorder (also called dissociative identity disorder or DID), and even some cases of schizophrenia can be the secondary results of traumatic events. While chronic pain usually has a physical origin, psychological factors frequently figure into the mix, since mind and body are not separate. Often the events that lead to physical pain are traumatic. Over time, physical pain itself can impair your life, leading to emotional reactions such as anxiety and depression. Regardless of the psychological or physical condition, treating the trauma is often an essential preliminary step in resolving both the secondary psychological problems as well as the primary psychological and physical condition.

Personal Loss

I'm no stranger to trauma. Since you're reading this book, that's also probably true of you or someone you care about. For me, trauma began at a very young age. When I was eleven, my mother was diagnosed with breast cancer. Then lymphoma raged throughout her body, ending her life in 1959 at age forty-three and leaving behind her loving husband and five children. I'm the oldest and I was only twelve when she died. I watched and listened helplessly as my passionate and vibrant mother withered away in agony. She suffered immensely, and we who loved her suffered too. You see, in those days, cancer patients mostly remained at home to the bitter end. Insufficient pain medication meant intense physical and emotional pain. We didn't have chemotherapy in those days, so my mother underwent multiple surgeries and radiation treatments that burned both cancer cells and healthy ones. I heard and saw her suffering—her expressions, moans, and tears. She had a little gold-colored bell that she rang when she needed help as she lay in her bed. At times, I was the one available to help her, if the rest of my family was away for part of the evening. I remember one time when I didn't hear the bell as soon as I should have. When I finally heard it and went to see what she needed, she sighed and said that she had been ringing the bell for a long time. I felt tremendously sad and guilty for not listening well enough, for getting caught up in what I was doing at the time. She didn't scold me; I scolded myself.

A year before her death, my father told me that she was going to die, and he asked me to guard the secret. She wasn't supposed to know that she was going to die or, if she did, at least she wasn't supposed to know that I knew. I don't know how we fooled ourselves into believing in this secret, but regardless I guarded the secret except for rare talks with my father. And she kept the secret too; she didn't talk to me about her condition and her fate either. It wasn't until the day the ambulance took her to the hospital for the final time that I realized that she knew. She kissed us children and told us to "be good." As I looked into her eyes, it was clear that we both understood. And I think we both knew that this would be the last time we would see each other in this life.

I did talk to God about my mother, and I prayed that she would be cured or at least that her misery would ease. Often I cried myself to sleep while praying. As a good Catholic boy, I even tried to relieve her pain by placing a holy scapular at various locations of her pain. She told me that it helped, but the pain relentlessly traveled throughout her body; there was no keeping up with it. I felt dejected, helpless, and hopeless, and I was convinced that my efforts did not help, even though in some ways they did. I believe now that she found some comfort, and even some pain relief, in my attempts.

There were many traumatic events surrounding my mother's death and each resulted in ongoing emotional distress for me. Although I was tormented, my three brothers and my sister also suffered. However, up to the point of her death, my father and I kept the secret from my siblings, which was probably best given their young ages. No doubt our father's heartbreak was the greatest of all, although I couldn't understand that at the time. I was more aware of my own loss, my own pain.

I recall the strong electrical charge—the bolt of lightning—that surged through my body when my father told me that she was going to die. They had just returned from the hospital, where she was receiving radiation treatment. I was making my brothers' beds and my father entered the room to talk with me. "I have to tell you something," he said with hesitation in his voice.

I looked at him, thinking that he was going to tell me to do more around the house. "I know," I whined. "Mom's sick and I need to help out. Can't you see I'm making the beds?"

"No, that's not it. I know you're helping a lot," he said with a solemn tone. "We just saw the doctor. And the doctor said …" He hesitated. "The doctor says that Mommy's going to die."

All I recall of that moment is that surge of electricity through my body, a feeling of fear, and the sensation of blood rushing out of my face. I was literally shocked. Then I felt numb and weak. I dropped to my knees for a moment. Actually my entire body felt drained of life energy. And then I slowly rose and walked toward the door, oblivious to anything but the numb feeling and sense of unreality. Any remaining hopes were dashed to the ground.

Then my father called to me. I turned and ran toward him, held on to him, and cried. He held me, and after a few minutes, he told me not to let Mom see me crying, that I had to be strong.

For me, my mother's illness and death were both agonizing and numbing. And these traumas interfered with my relationships for many years to come. My grief was complex, and I tried to cope by not thinking about it, by telling myself that it was long ago, and sometimes by emotionally reliving the painful events that occurred before and after her death. But ultimately none of this helped. I don't think it occurred to me that my grief could be eliminated by anything other than the passage of time, if then. Yet time was not healing these wounds, and I had to wait three decades for relief through other means. Amazingly the resolution of many of these traumas took only a few minutes. How can this be? Initially I found it extremely difficult to believe that something I suffered from for so long could be resolved so quickly. Yet now this has become common sense to me, to many of the people I treat, and to the professionals I teach. In this book, I discuss how trauma sufferers can be helped quickly through these simple techniques and understandings—just as I was helped. I shall show you how to effectively apply these techniques on your own. Before we get to that, however, let me tell you about another traumatic event that illustrates some other considerations that are important in resolving trauma.

My Automobile Accident

I was twenty-one and just graduated from Duquesne University in Pittsburgh, Pennsylvania, where I majored in the three Ps: philosophy, psychology, and parties. The day after graduation, I had an automobile accident that nearly claimed my life. It was early June 1968. I was driving my red Volkswagen beetle to the university's student union to meet friends when a car much larger than mine—I believe it was a Chevy—ripped off my driver's door. The crash sent me flying through the air, in what seemed to be slow motion, into some wooden steps that broke from the impact of my body. Then I bounced over a banister, slid along the sidewalk, and rolled over before coming to an abrupt stop. It was hot and dusty. Immediately I tried to get up, and at that moment I could feel that I was bleeding inside. I rolled over and looked up at the sky, terrified that I was going to die. I shouted, "No! I'm not going to die! I'm not ready." I believe that affirmation and my determination were keys to my survival.

I remember the man who was driving the other car, which came to a screeching stop (what seemed like a long time after I stopped sliding). He seemed frantic and traumatized as he rushed to me lying on the sidewalk. Out of his distress, he shouted that he just had bodywork done on his car and now the paint job was ruined. He seemed to "stutter" back and forth between me and his car in confusion, until I firmly shouted for him to help me or leave. That brought him to his senses and he came to my aid.

People were running from all directions toward the scene. A young woman came out of her house, rushed over, put a pillow under my head, and covered me with a blanket. I told her she was beautiful and must be an angel. My shoes had come off my feet as I flew through the air, and I asked the people that encircled me to please find them. My car radio was on, and the song that was playing seemed horrid to me. "I hate that song," I said. "Would someone please shut off the radio?" Somebody went over and clicked it off. "Thank you," I sighed in relief.

The ambulance rushed me to Mercy Hospital, just around the corner. I had many injuries, including a ruptured spleen. I underwent surgery and received six pints of blood. My life hung in the balance for several days. I was in the intensive care unit for the first four days and in the hospital for ten days altogether. During that time, I was given morphine and I developed a dependence on that euphoric sensation that morphine can give you. Regardless of the temptation, I never turned to morphine after recovering.

For three months after the accident, I recovered at home. During that time, I also had thyroid surgery. Even though my physical condition improved quickly after the surgeries, I continued to experience psychological effects for many years: fear when I was driving, anxiety, flashbacks, and frequent episodes of panic with the feeling that I was going to die. So, as a result of that trauma, complicated by the previous traumas related to my mother's death, I suffered from PTSD, generalized anxiety, panic disorder, and phobia.

I resolved these conditions over a period of time by learning to relax my hold on the steering wheel while driving, and by riding out a severe panic attack one evening about eight years after the accident. Back then, I had many panic attacks, but this one continued for over two hours. I tried everything I could think of to settle the panic: walking around the house wringing my hands, soaking my head in water, taking a warm shower, taking a cold shower, quickly downing a shot of whiskey, breathing deeply into a paper bag, running down the street and back, trying to console myself with rational self-talk, and more. Finally I became disgusted and angry with the panic and, oddly enough, I tried to intensify it. I closed my eyes and focused on the panic sensations—into the abyss, so to speak. With defiance, I spoke to the panic, "Come on and get me!"

The curious result was the complete opposite; the panic instantly vanished. I had come face-to-face with my fear, stared it straight in the eye, did not waver, and the panic fled. I think I might have scared it away. About a week later, another panic attack started. I simply faced it and tried to go into it and magnify it. And again, it instantly disappeared. I searched for any inkling of panic or anxiety in my body, but it was gone. I'm pretty sure that I scared that one away too. What satisfaction I felt about this serendipitous discovery! From then on, I no longer lived in dread of panic. If a twinge of anxiety occurred, I faced it, observed it, tried to intensify it, and it would vanish. I also knew that I could not use this approach in an attempt to outwit panic, since the panic would surely know. I couldn't pretend that I was accepting and attempting to intensify the panic, since that would be just another attempt to avoid or escape it. I had to really accept it and aim to intensify it! After all, the panic and my own awareness were not separate. I had to truly want to immerse myself in it, no matter what. The immersion had to be for real. Later I learned that what I did was essentially "paradoxical intention," a technique that Viktor Frankl wrote about in *Man's Search for Meaning* (1959). Paradoxical intention involves consciously trying to make an uncomfortable or frightening symptom occur that you would logically prefer to eliminate. As a result, it generally becomes difficult or impossible to experience the symptom.

My confidence grew and I came to understand the sources of my panic, which was partly about a blind spot in my awareness—something that I concluded while I was flying out of my car in June 1968. As I hit the sidewalk, I had the rather detached thought, "Am I going to die now or after I stop sliding?" It was not a matter of if I was going to die; dying was assumed. It was just a matter of how soon. When I stopped sliding along the sidewalk, my death was inevitable and imminent. The panic always carried with it the sense that I was going to die now and I had to fight to stay alive. While it was certainly good to decide not to die at the time of the accident, somehow I took this out of context. In a sense, the accident and dying were ever present, or nearly so. Traumatic stress is created the moment we say no to the present moment and the flow of life energy is blocked along with important aspects of our awareness. The ancient Chinese called it stagnant qi (pronounced chee, as in cheese).

Eventually I understood that panic—that strong electrical (energy) charge—was also connected to my mother's death and dying. Remember the electrical charge I experienced when my father told me that my mother was going to die? Well, here it was again in other contexts. So basically the trauma and panic were energetic. To some, resolution of a trauma can be a long, drawn-out process, but when an effective method is applied, very little time is needed. While I was able to use acceptance and intensification to overcome panic, it was not until about sixteen years later that I came upon cutting-edge methods of treating trauma—what I later called energy psychology and energy tapping. It was through this approach, which is the centerpiece of this book, that I was able to completely eliminate traumas and other problems that had plagued me for so many years.

This book goes into great detail about effective methods of alleviating the blocked energy that accounts for trauma. However, before we get into that, let's first review some additional information about trauma.

Releasing Our Attachment to Trauma

Siddhārtha Gautama, better known as Buddha, said that life is suffering due to strong desire or attachments, and that cessation of suffering is attainable. While some level of attachment seems to be healthy and good, such as loving someone, since you can only briefly have anything, becoming too attached makes suffering possible. Trauma is so prevalent that we might revise Buddha's maxim and conclude that life is suffering because of trauma. Trauma, however, is not only about awful events but also about our attachment in the aftermath of those events. Attachment at many levels accounts for trauma.

Obviously there is a difference between a traumatic event and the traumatic memory. The memory is merely a reflection of what happened in the past. However, not so obvious is the distinction between the traumatic memory and traumatic stress or trauma. It seems as though the memory causes the distress, but this is not the case. This will become quite clear as you read this book and apply the intervention exercises.

While there is a conscious attachment to the memory of the traumatic event and its meaning or the meaning you give it, trauma also involves an unconscious attachment. That unconscious attachment fuels trauma not so much by what you remember as by what you have forgotten. So trauma is about forgetting or being unaware of certain information. Because you have forgotten it or are unaware of it, you therefore are not able to come to terms with it. This is the basis of Freud's psychoanalysis, which emphasizes that psychological problems are the result of unconscious issues, and that effective and deep treatment involves bringing the unconscious into conscious awareness. The goal of psychoanalysis is to help the patient thoroughly uncover and process or work through the unconscious material involved in the trauma. Psychoanalysis and other methods based on this understanding involve archeological expeditions to unearth the lost details of the memory so that the unfinished business can be finished. In short, there is something subliminal or concealed about the memory, and that gives it power to trigger emotional and physical distress. Once you have insight into the unconscious basis of the problem, which really involves thoughts at an unconscious level, those thoughts no longer have power over you. As the saying goes, "The truth shall set you free."

Even though this formulation appears to be accurate, many people become traumatized during attempts to uncover and review the details of the traumatic event. So trauma can build on trauma, resulting in a chronic condition. The strong emotional upset that may occur during therapy of this nature has been described as retraumatization. That is, the upset of reviewing the traumatic event can be traumatic too. I have found, however, that it is not necessary to go through emotional upheaval in order to resolve trauma. It is possible to review the traumatic event in such a way that the pieces of the puzzle are filled in without having to go through any distress (or only a very little distress) in the process. Frequently it is not even necessary to review the traumatic event in order to experience ongoing relief from traumatic stress. These highly effective ways of relieving trauma are covered in this book. But before we focus on these cutting-edge ways of treating trauma, especially energy tapping, let's take a closer look at some customary ways that trauma is being treated today.

2

Customary Treatments for Trauma

People are not disturbed by things, but by the view they take of them.

—Epictetus

Trauma and post-traumatic stress disorder (PTSD) have existed since the dawn of civilization. It's quite possible that only human beings and domesticated animals can develop these conditions, since creatures in the wild seem to resolve trauma efficiently through natural mechanisms such as bodily shaking and completing what they started before the traumatic episode stopped them (Levin 1997). Escape and the ability to fight back also help to prevent the development of trauma, while helplessly freezing in your tracks is an essential aspect of locking in trauma. It would seem that being civilized is a double-edged sword, since maintaining a record of traumatic events ensures survival as well as suffering. Nature seems to be more dedicated to survival of the species than to comfort of the individual.

A Brief History of Trauma Treatment

The PTSD diagnosis first appeared in 1980 in the third edition of the *Diagnostic and Statistical Manual of Mental Disorders* (*DSM-III*), with the preceding two editions using the terms "stress response syndrome" (*DSM-II*) and "situational disorders" (*DSM-I*). This problem, however, is not new. It has been described, using other names, for millennia. For example, the ancient Egyptians and Greeks wrote about warriors who suffered emotionally from combat. During the American Civil War, PTSD was referred to as "soldier's heart," during World War I as "shell shock" or the "effort syndrome," and during World War II as "combat fatigue." Recently a further distinction has been made about a more severe and recalcitrant form of PTSD: complex PTSD or disorders of extreme stress (DES). This condition highlights the lasting personality changes as a result of traumatic experiences on some survivors.

In chapter 1, we talked about psychoanalysis, which involves recalling the repressed or forgotten details of the traumatic event. The goal of psychoanalysis is to help you become conscious of information that has remained hidden in your unconscious. This is called insight (in-sight or seeing within). However, the methods used in psychoanalysis—free association, dream analysis, and interpretation—are better suited for other trauma-based conditions, such as phobias and hysteria, which is referred to as "conversion reaction" or "conversion disorder" today. Conversion disorder involves symptoms such as paralysis or blindness that do not have a physical cause but are the result of trauma and psychological conflict. The symptoms are unconscious attempts to resolve the conflict. Nonetheless, brief psychodynamic psychotherapy, a modern approach that is related to psychoanalysis, is helpful in treating trauma-based disorders. This approach helps you understand the unconscious meaning of your PTSD symptoms or other trauma-based symptoms and helps you cope.

A more ancient perspective about trauma—that of the shaman—is that a person's soul or part of the soul leaves the body when a traumatic event occurs. The shaman goes into an altered state and travels to find the dislodged or lost soul (which may be near the body, or in the under- or upper-world) and escort it back into the body. This is called "soul retrieval." While this viewpoint seems odd to us and modern psychology has a different view of the shaman's techniques, shamanic approaches often prove effective and shamans are still in business today.

During WW II, treatment for traumatized soldiers involved "catharsis" (relieving tension and anxiety by bringing repressed memories, thoughts, and feelings to consciousness) while revisiting or reliving the traumatic events. This is also referred to as "abreaction." Other methods included reviewing repressed memories during hypnosis or being interviewed after being injected with sodium amytal (narcosynthesis). Sodium amytal is a barbiturate that causes drowsiness and sleep by increasing the actions of gamma-aminobutyric acid (GABA), an inhibitory or sedating neurotransmitter. A neurotransmitter is a chemical that relays and modulates electrical impulses between neurons and other cells. After being treated with these methods, soldiers were given a brief rest before rejoining their comrades on the front lines (Herman 1992).

The nervous system is divided into the *sympathetic* (alert) and *parasympathetic* (calm) nervous systems. PTSD results in being chronically on alert (sympathetic), so increasing GABA reduces sympathetic activity or hyperarousal. Sodium amytal sometimes makes it possible to review the traumatic events and resolve the trauma without becoming unduly emotionally upset in the process. Hypnosis and sodium amytal interviews reduced resistance and made it possible to recall the details of traumatic events with some degree of emotional insulation. Recalling and reliving details of the traumatic event remains an essential feature of many current therapeutic approaches, although some significant modifications have been introduced over time.

Medication and Trauma

Various psychotropic (psychiatric) medications are often used as an adjunct in the treatment of PTSD and other trauma-based conditions. While these medications do not cure trauma, they often help to reduce symptoms and in some cases may improve the effectiveness of psychological treatment. They also help reduce emotional upset during some therapeutic methods, such as "flooding." Flooding involves emotionally reliving a traumatic event. While some people choose to remain on medication without psychological treatment, I believe this is ill advised. Many mental health professionals believe that the combination of therapy and medication often improves the likelihood of recovery.

Chemistry and Trauma

Traumatic stress is accompanied by the release of various chemicals in your body: cortisol, oxytocin, vasopressin, endogenous opioids, epinephrine, and norepinephrine. Also a low level of serotonin, an important neurotransmitter, is instrumental in exaggerated startle response (Depue and Spoont 1986), suicide and aggression (Coccaro et al. 1989), and preoccupation with the traumatic event (van der Kolk and van der Hart 1991). This neurotransmitter is also implicated in depression and obsessive-compulsive disorder (Jenike and Rauch 1994).

Neurotransmitters

The nervous system, and our bodies as a whole, requires electrical energy in order to work. *Neurotransmitters* are important chemicals that operate at synapses (little spaces) between neurons (nerve cells) and transfer electrical signals and information throughout the nervous system and body. Synapses are junctions that allow neurons to form interconnected circuits. These interconnected circuits are essential to perception and thought, and they also provide the means by which the nervous system connects to and controls muscles, glands, and other systems of the body. Some scientists believe that personality, or the "self," is the result of interconnected synapses (LeDoux 2002).

The average number of neurons in the human brain is one hundred billion. It is estimated that young children may have as many as a trillion synapses. By the time you become an adult, however, the range is trimmed to about one hundred million to five hundred million synapses. Apparently if you don't use it, you lose it. When the level of neurotransmitters contained within the synapses is adequate, there is a healthy flow of information signals and your mind and body operate well. If the amount of certain neurotransmitters is significantly reduced or depleted, physical problems and emotional distress in the form of anxiety, depression, and obsession may result.

Serotonin and SSRIs

As noted, an imbalance of serotonin (a molecule) occurs with depression, anxiety, and trauma symptoms, including avoidance and hypervigilance. Zoloft (sertraline) is one medication approved by the Food and Drug Administration (FDA) for the treatment of PTSD. Zoloft is a selective serotonin reuptake inhibitor (SSRI), a chemical agent (molecule) that helps the brain to maintain adequate levels of serotonin. It is therefore often effective in reducing many trauma symptoms such as obsessive thoughts, avoidance, and insomnia. Other SSRIs such as Luvox (fluvoxamine), Prozac (fluoxetine), and Paxil (paroxetine) are also prescribed for such purposes. The earliest cousin of the SSRIs, Desyrel (trazodone), has SSRI qualities and is also used to promote sleep and reduce nightmares. Side effects of SSRIs are generally minimal but may include nausea, drowsiness, headache, change in weight and appetite, lower sexual desire, and delayed orgasm. It should be noted that in addition to increasing serotonin, these medications appear to promote the growth of neurons and synapses. So the overall effect is not limited to chemistry.

Tricyclic and Tetracyclic Antidepressants (TCAs)

Prior to the development of SSRIs and other new-generation antidepressants, tricyclic and tetracyclic antidepressants (TCAs) were more frequently used to treat depression, anxiety, and trauma symptoms. They still remain viable choices for patients with severe depression who do not respond adequately to the newer medications. TCAs generally do not help the brain to maintain higher levels of serotonin. They increase instead the availability of other neurotransmitters such as norepinephrine and dopamine. These neurotransmitters are important for attention and focus.

TCAs are not as effective in reducing PTSD symptoms of flashbacks, avoidance, and hyperarousal. Additionally they may result in side effects such as dry mouth, stomach upset, urinary retention, constipation, blurred vision, fatigue, tremors, and orthostatic hypotension (drop in blood pressure upon standing that results in dizziness, faintness, or light-headedness). Among the most frequently prescribed medications in this class are Elavil (amitriptyline), Norpramin (desipramine), Pamelor (nortriptyline), Sinequan (doxepin), and Tofranil (imipramine). Remeron (mirtazapine) and Ludiomil (maprotiline) are tetracyclic antidepressants that are frequently prescribed for depression and insomnia.

Monoamine Oxidase Inhibitors (MAOIs)

Monoamine oxidase inhibitors (MAOIs), such as Nardil (phenelzine), Marplan (isocarboxazid), and Parnate (tranylcypromine), interfere with the production of monoamine oxidase, an enzyme that destroys serotonin and other neurotransmitters. MAOIs have been used primarily to treat severe intractable depression, but they are seldom used today because of dangerous side effects, such as rapidly elevating blood pressure (hypertensive crisis) in patients whose diets contain tyramine. Tyramine is found in various meats, fish, poultry, and eggs; foods that are aged, dried, fermented, salted, smoked, or pickled; soy and teriyaki sauces; nuts; alcoholic beverages; and mincemeat pie. Nardil has been shown to produce some improvement in flashbacks, avoidance, nightmares, and insomnia, although it does not reduce hyperarousal. However, since many people suffering from PTSD may turn to alcohol and other substances for "self-medication," there are significant risks involved with taking an MAOI.

Anti-Adrenergic Medications

There are a number of other medications used to treat PTSD symptoms. Anti-adrenergic agents, such as Catapres (clonidine) and Inderal (propranolol), can help to reduce nightmares, hypervigilance, startle reactions, and rage. These medications are also used to treat hypertension, cardiac arrhythmias, angina pectoris, glaucoma, and migraine headaches.

Tranquilizers

Benzodiazepines are medications commonly known as tranquilizers and sleeping pills. While there are no controlled studies proving the effectiveness of benzodiazepines in the treatment of PTSD, short-term usage of these medications is often helpful in reducing anxiety, insomnia, and irritability. Valium (diazepam), Xanax (alprazolam), Ativan (lorazepam), and Klonopin (clonazepam) are benzodiazepines. However, there is the risk of dependence and withdrawal symptoms with these tranquilizers. One tranquilizer that has been touted as not causing dependence, withdrawal symptoms, or side effects such as dizziness is BuSpar (buspirone). Nonetheless, precaution with even this medication is advised.

Mood Stabilizers

Other medications used in the treatment of PTSD and many other psychiatric conditions include mood stabilizers such as Eskalith (lithium carbonate), Depakote (divalproex sodium), Lamictal (lamotrigine), Neurontin (gabapentin), and Topamax (topiramate). These medications are primarily used with bipolar and some other disorders.

Newer Antidepressants

A new class of medication called selective serotonin and norepinephrine reuptake inhibitors (SSNRIs) combines the effects of TCAs and SSRIs. Cymbalta (duloxetine) is an SSNRI. Wellbutrin (bupropion) is a serotonin, norepinephrine, and dopamine reuptake inhibitor (SNDRI). And the list of molecules marches on.

Alternative Substances

Certain amino acids and fatty acids can help replenish serotonin, dopamine, norepinephrine, and other neurotransmitters. The essential amino acid L-tryptophan (which you can get from milk and turkey) and omega-3 and omega-9 fatty acids (which you can get from some fatty fish and flaxseed oil) are useful in this respect. Research-grade Saint-John's-wort (*Hypericum perforatum*) has also been shown by some studies to be effective in treating mild to moderate depression and anxiety by reducing the reuptake of serotonin, dopamine, and norepinephrine. So in some respects Saint-John's-wort functions like an SNDRI. There are many other supplements that are used to treat depression and other trauma symptoms, including certain flower essences. However, most of these alternatives do not have a solid research base.

As we close this section, it should be noted that many medications and techniques are used even though we do not know exactly how and why they work. A frequent statement in the *Physicians' Desk Reference* (*PDR*) is that "the mechanism of action remains to be fully elucidated." While medications undergo multimillion-dollar drug trials before receiving FDA approval, we never really know the far-reaching effects of a medication until it has been extensively prescribed in real-life situations. After an accumulation of positive and negative experiences in the field, further indications and precautions are published, or perhaps the medication is recalled.

Currently there is much debate about the advisability of using various psychotropic medications with children, since research has not demonstrated their effectiveness with children. Before a medication is made available for treatment, it is generally researched on animals and adults but seldom, if ever, on children.

Neuroscience

When you experience a traumatic event and continue to suffer traumatic stress, obviously significant effects are occurring in your body. There is evidence that certain anatomical structures in the subcortical limbic system of the brain are significantly activated during a traumatic event and perpetuate traumatic stress.

One of these structures is the *amygdala*, an almond-shaped set of nerve cells (neurons) deep in the brain's medial temporal lobe that is intricately involved in processing emotions, especially fear and pleasure. The amygdala is a kind of scout that keeps an eye out for danger and is instrumental in the fight-flight-freeze response. That is, it helps you to survive by fighting, running, or playing dead. When a traumatic event occurs, your amygdala gets activated. Even after the traumatic event is over, it will often become triggered at anything that even remotely reminds you of the traumatic event.

A second structure to consider is the *hippocampus*, a seahorse-shaped structure (*hippokampos* is Greek for seahorse) located in the temporal lobes of the brain. You have two of them, and they are instrumental in memory and navigation. The hippocampus lets you know that something is in the past—just a memory. However, when the amygdala becomes overcharged due to trauma, in a sense the hippocampus becomes disabled. The trauma is then experienced as ever present rather than in the past. In this sense, the goal of therapy is to calm the amygdala and allow the hippocampus to record the traumatic event as over—as just a memory.

Behavior Therapy

To lay the groundwork for our discussion of behavior therapy, I'd like to share two stories. First, when I was about eight years old, I had an especially nauseating experience. My dad was using a noxious-smelling paint on the basement floor and of course I was right down there helping him. Soon I became light-headed and he made me go upstairs to get away from the fumes.

Shortly afterward I got a strong craving for peas. I simply loved peas in those days! So I asked my dad if he would cook some for me. He opened a can and poured them into a bowl, insisting that they were already cooked. I was hoping for deep green-colored peas, but these peas were a yellow-green, not-very-appetizing variety. And I wanted them heated up, like Mom did. So he put them in a pan and heated them for about a minute. Although my father was highly accomplished in repairing refrigeration systems (and maybe even painting basement floors), he was not a culinary artist. Yet I ate the faded lukewarm peas anyway.

Not very long after consuming those yellow-green little spheres, I became extremely nauseated. Probably it was the fumes that got to me, although I also wasn't used to eating lukewarm peas out of a can. Anyway, I rushed to the bathroom and vomited all those now quite mushy peas into the toilet. After that, I couldn't stand the sight, smell, or even mention of peas! Not even the dark-green variety that I preferred. My sister loved to tease me and trigger my conditioned response. I remember her calling my name and putting a spoonful of peas in her mouth in front of me, which promptly made me gag. Eventually I outgrew this conditioned response to peas, partly because I remembered how much I used to love peas, and also since my sister was so unrelenting in tormenting me. Somehow her constant agitation eventually eliminated my nauseated response to peas. But to my sister's glee, that took about six years!

The second story occurred long before my encounter with those peas. In the early 1900s, Russian physiologist Ivan Pavlov did some interesting experiments with dogs that demonstrated conditioning. You know the story about Pavlov's dogs. He was studying the mechanisms of salivation and observed that the dogs in his experiments drooled even when they were not being exposed to food, which is not at all uncommon for dogs. Interestingly, however, he found that the dogs drooled simply when seeing the experimenters who wore white lab coats. And he discovered that simply showing them white lab coats was sufficient to induce drooling. Next he trained his dogs to salivate to the sound of a bell. I gather that might have really confused them: "Why are we drooling at the sound of a bell? Where's the beef?" He did this by ringing a bell while they were salivating at the sight and smell of food. Presto: conditioned response! Basically a natural reflex or unconditioned response, such as salivating or being startled after hearing a loud noise, is associated with something that doesn't normally cause the natural reflex. This is what happened with me when I became nauseated about peas. Nausea occurred right after I ate peas and the sight of the peas in the toilet after vomiting reinforced the pea-nausea association even further.

Behavior therapy is based on principles of conditioning and, in particular, how to extinguish unwanted conditioning and install desired conditioning. When you have a traumatic experience and it really sticks, you're adversely conditioned: the experience, consciously and unconsciously, replays in your mind and body. Many things (stimuli) can trigger the memory and the emotional distress associated with the traumatic event.

If you have PTSD, a behavior therapist would help you to determine the various situations (stimuli) that trigger the various symptoms (responses), which might be flashbacks, nightmares, hypervigilance, heightened startle response, affective numbing, or any number of other responses. The stimuli might include situations, objects, and/or thoughts that remind you of the traumatic event. For example, in the case of Pavlov's dogs, the stimulus was the bell that induced salivation. The stimulus-response (S-R) bonds are then the basis of treatment efforts. Essentially behavior therapists consider the problem to be a matter of conditioning or learning. Extinction or elimination of the distressing S-R bonds is the goal of therapy.

One behavioral technique involves exposing you to various triggers in imagination or in vivo (that is, exposing you to the actual trigger—peas, in my case) while preventing avoidance. This is called *flooding*, or emotional reliving, and it eventually results in extinction of the symptoms. Recall my experience with the peas. Given repeated exposure to peas from my sister and other family members, my nausea at the sight, thought, or smell of peas eventually disappeared. Escaping the emotional reaction by dissociating or avoiding stimuli that trigger the emotional reaction actually strengthens the S-R bond, since escaping such situations is a kind of pleasure and is reinforcing. This is called "negative reinforcement."

Dr. Joseph Wolpe (1958) developed *systematic desensitization*, a technique that makes the exposure and extinction process less painful. This is accomplished by the following:

1. Construct a hierarchy from the least to the most anxiety-provoking images related to the traumatic event or phobia.

2. Introduce a state of deep relaxation via progressive relaxation. This is accomplished through deep breathing and tightening and relaxing various muscle groups throughout your body.

3. Picture the least upsetting image while maintaining relaxation until you are able to effortlessly feel relaxed while picturing the image.

4. Move on to the next more upsetting image and so on until the entire trauma or phobia is neutralized.

Relaxation inhibits the anxiety connected to the various triggers, including the memory of the trauma. Dr. Wolpe correctly assumed that anxiety and relaxation are mutually exclusive: "If a response inhibitory to anxiety can be made to occur in the presence of anxiety-evoking stimuli so that it is accompanied by a complete or partial suppression of the anxiety response, the bond between these stimuli and the anxiety response will be weakened" (Wolpe 1961, 189). This is called *reciprocal inhibition*. In some cases, such as the treatment of phobias, this technique can also be done in the presence of the feared object, what is called "in vivo exposure," rather than through internal imagery.

Exposure therapies, including flooding and systematic desensitization, reduce PTSD anxiety symptoms (Boudewyns and Hyer 1990; Foa et al. 1991; Cooper and Clum 1989; Keane et al. 1989), although exposure can also result in panic episodes, depression, and relapse in people who have been alcohol dependent (Pitman et al. 1991). Usually many exposure sessions (sixty to ninety minutes long) are needed before the trauma can be relieved, with the most significant results occurring after fifteen sessions (Brom, Klebar, and Defares 1989).

Cognitive Behavioral Therapy

Another popular approach to the treatment of PTSD and many other conditions is *cognitive therapy*, which involves recognizing and changing disturbing thoughts. However, today cognitive therapy and behavior therapy are usually combined in the form of *cognitive behavioral therapy* (CBT). CBT focuses on directly challenging your disturbing thinking and behavior by engineering experiments that confront the problem. For example, if you fell off a ladder and developed a phobia of climbing ladders, CBT would involve helping you to dispute any irrational thinking that contributes to the phobia and also help you rapidly or gradually return to climbing ladders. Since my early days as a counselor and then psychologist, I have used CBT principles to help people resolve trauma, depression, phobias, anxiety disorders, and addiction.

While the behavior therapist looks at the relationship between the situation (environment) and behavior (including symptoms), the cognitive therapist focuses on internal causes of behavior and symptoms. These internal causes are thoughts, which also include memories and beliefs. In this view, thoughts, not simply the environmental situation, are the most significant factors involved in the emotional upset. Internal self-talk, beliefs, and other internal processes, such as images, are important aspects of your emotional distress. As far as internal imagery is concerned, the degree of distress may be the result of how vivid, colorful, and lifelike the image or "movie" is.

There are many varieties of CBT. One example is rational emotive behavior therapy (REBT), developed by Dr. Albert Ellis. This approach assists you in categorizing and challenging thoughts and behaviors associated with anxiety, depression, addiction, personality disorders, and others. REBT teaches you to recognize that your disturbance is the result of "awfulizing" or engaging in catastrophic thinking, and teaches you how to dispute these thoughts and irrational beliefs. According to Ellis, it is not the circumstance that causes the distress but rather the irrational belief. Irrational beliefs include notions like the following:

- It is absolutely necessary for you to be loved by significant others for almost everything you do.

- It is horrible when things are not as you would like them to be.

- Your misery is externally caused and is forced on you by outside people and events.

- If something is or may be dangerous or fearsome, you should be terribly upset and obsessed about it.

It is possible to recognize the fallacy of these beliefs and to challenge them so that they have less of a hold on you. REBT includes forceful disputing of the irrational belief through both logic and behavioral exercises, such as confronting your fears. You can affect your own internal processing and behavior so that you can have power over things outside of you.

CBT helps you to observe the internal movie and narrative that you engage in, which is how the psychological experience is created. With this approach, you are assisted in altering your emotional response by changing how you label it. For example, instead of labeling the event as awful and seeing yourself as damaged because of it, your emotional reaction will be significantly changed if you come to consistently and congruently see it as a learning experience in which you survived and became stronger.

Of course, CBT might focus on internal processes other than beliefs and narration. For example, altering the tone of your internal voice from desperation to confidence and calm would produce a shift in your emotional response. Also, where you place an internal image in your visual field can make a difference. Try it.

1. Think about something that happened that is somewhat upsetting. Notice where in your visual field it is located. Is it straight ahead? To the right or left? Up or down?

2. Now change its location. Actually move it in your visual field. Does that change the way you feel?

3. Try another location. How does that feel?

4. If this works for you, learning to consistently move the picture to that area of your visual field where you feel best can help you to manage and perhaps resolve the distress of this event. You can also do this with internal sounds by changing the tone and location of your mental voice as you internally talk about or narrate the event. For example, a frightening thought might not have the same impact if it is spoken like Donald Duck or Mickey Mouse.

Another way to approach this issue of thought and disturbance is to simply notice your feelings. When you feel good, your thoughts are healthy. When you feel angry, depressed, or anxious, your thoughts are dis-eased. That is, they *disturb* the *ease* of your mind and body. Think of your feelings as an internal barometer that gives you information about the quality of your thinking and perceiving. It's not that the feelings are necessarily the truth; they simply reflect your thoughts. And thoughts can be mistaken. So it's not necessary to examine and dispute the thoughts. You can just let them go. Thought is not independently powerful, separate from the power that you give it.

Group Therapy

Group therapy is often used to help trauma survivors. It is more economical and provides opportunities for the group members to share about their traumatic events and the symptoms in a safe and supportive environment. The process often has a cognitive behavioral focus and includes an educational component. As group members discuss and share how they cope with trauma-related emotional reactions such as shame, guilt, and self-condemnation, this often makes it possible to focus more on the present rather than living in the past. I find that it is important to not spend too much time focusing on the problem in group therapy, since such focus can sometimes be retraumatizing and can also reinforce identification of oneself as a victim or trauma survivor. It is far better to spend most of the time emphasizing positive aspects, such as your inner strengths and goals.

Family Therapy

Family therapy is often an important aspect of healing trauma. It may involve sessions with the entire family or specific relationships, such as husband-wife, brother-sister, mother-daughter, or father-son. Family therapy can emphasize helping the traumatized member to recover, dealing with how the traumatized member has affected others, and sometimes changing the entire family system as a whole. The emphasis will vary depending upon the health and coping strategies of the family prior to the traumatic event. If the event is recent, the effects and focus may be limited to the traumatized member. The longer the family has lived with a traumatized member, the more likely the other members will be affected. If the traumatized family member's symptoms have become chronic, the entire family may be affected and then treatment is directed at the entire family system.

The same logic for group therapy also applies to family therapy. It is important to not spend too much of the time focusing on the problem, since this can be retraumatizing and also reinforce the role as victim. It is far better to emphasize positive aspects, such as your inner strengths and goals.

What Else?

Recently a number of complementary and alternative psychotherapies (CAPs) have entered the mainstream. These approaches are not yet widely used, but history tells us that it's just a matter of time. Basically that's what happened with psychotropic (psychiatric) medication and CBT. When they first came on the scene, these approaches to treatment were ridiculed; eventually they became widely accepted as common sense. As you will learn in the next chapter, these newer complementary and alternative approaches often work much more rapidly than the customary approaches, although integrating these therapies with more traditional treatment is often advisable. Let's explore these complementary and alternative therapies now.

3

Complementary and Alternative Treatments for Trauma

All truth goes through three stages. First it's ridiculed, then it's opposed, and finally it's accepted as being self-evident.

—Schopenhauer

While customary treatments for trauma and PTSD are often effective, frequently weeks or months of treatment are needed before you feel better, and seldom is trauma considered to be "cured." Amelioration or improvement are the preferred terms in the fields of psychiatry and psychology. Based on neuroscientific evidence, there's a general belief that trauma remains indelibly imprinted in the brain. Even when all clinical signs of PTSD are alleviated, certain conditions and enough stress can often resurrect the trauma.

While psychological treatment is highly beneficial for all sorts of problems, usually rapid results are not the rule. Classical psychoanalysis, for example, can take years to produce results. The focus of psychoanalysis is insight, and insight doesn't necessarily eliminate symptoms. You might think that knowing the unconscious reasons for depression, anxiety, or traumatic symptoms would cure the problem, but instead it often simply results in a better understanding of the problem. Now that can be helpful, but you'd probably prefer to eliminate the problem.

Even many modern therapies do not produce quick results. Ordinarily a number of sessions are needed before you can be certain that you have benefited. Is this because resolving psychological problems requires extensive time and effort, or because many therapies are not up to the task of achieving results quickly?

Recently several techniques for trauma have been developed that frequently produce positive results in a matter of one or a few sessions (Carbonell and Figley 1999). While these approaches have many characteristics in common with standard therapies, they are unique. When a therapy produces quick and lasting results, well, we've just got to stop and take notice! So let's take a look.

Traumatic Incident Reduction (TIR)

One of these therapies, *traumatic incident reduction* (TIR), was developed by psychiatrist Frank Gerbode (1989). This is an exposure technique in which you choose a traumatic event that can be resolved within the course of a single session (which can take anywhere from thirty minutes to several hours). Initially you pay attention to what you were aware of just prior to the traumatic event and then you review the entire incident silently from beginning to end. Next you report what you observed. The process is repeated many times until you arrive at a resolution. TIR is based on the finding that there are gaps in your memory, and that by reviewing the event in detail, your mind fills in the gaps. As you become aware of the lost information, the negative emotions and thoughts associated with the event resolve. The intensity of the trauma is also frequently compounded by earlier related traumas that will be recalled during TIR.

Although TIR is similar to flooding, it is also different in many ways. While the behavior therapist may attend to his or her relationship with you, the TIR therapist takes great pains and spends the time necessary to establish a positive and supportive relationship. The therapist is nondirective rather than trying to get you to think differently about the event. It seems to be sufficient to review the trauma and discover your own resolution; however, similar to other forms of flooding, TIR may cause strong emotional reactions.

Visual-Kinesthetic Dissociation (V/KD)

Visual-kinesthetic dissociation (V/KD) was developed by Richard Bandler and John Grinder in the 1970s after studying the work of several renowned therapists, including psychiatrist Dr. Milton H. Erickson, MD (Bandler and Grinder 1979). V/KD is based on neutralizing stimulus-response (S-R) bonds between sensory systems (vision, hearing, smell, etc.). That is, an external or internal visual stimulus can result in an immediate painful or negative feeling (kinesthetic) response. For example, you might cringe if you imagine someone scratching his or her fingernails against a chalkboard. The imagining is the visual and the cringing is the kinesthetic response. V/KD eliminates the S-R bond by introducing detachment (dissociation) while you re-view the traumatic memory. Essentially dissociation is inserted between the visual stimulus and the kinesthetic response. This causes the S-R bond to become extinct. That is, since you no longer recall the trauma in an "associated manner"—as if you are reexperiencing it "in the flesh"—negative emotion is removed from the memory. V/KD causes a shift in your recall of the memory from "associated," or reliving the experience, to "dis-associated," or viewing it from a position of not being involved. V/KD combines elements of exposure, hypnosis, guided imagery, cognitive therapy, and reciprocal inhibition (that is, you can't feel relaxed and anxious at the same time). I used V/KD with Carol, a client who had been traumatized by a car accident.

■ *Carol's Story*

While driving to work early one morning, Carol, a thirty-five-year-old emergency room nurse, suffered a concussion and other injuries in a head-on collision. After recovering from her injuries, she was afraid to drive and also experienced considerable anxiety as a passenger. Because of this tremendous fear, she was unable to return to work. Despite her fear, Carol was not able to remember the details of her accident. This is common in cases of head injury (for assumed neurologic and neurochemical reasons). Eighteen months after the accident at the request of Carol's husband, I went to their home and took her through a technique to help her with this phobic reaction. We did this therapy in their kitchen, sitting at the kitchen table. Her husband, Tom, sat next to her throughout the treatment.

After explaining what we were going to do, I asked Carol to recall the last thing she remembered before the accident. She recalled getting into her car to go to work, as she did on any other work day. I had her picture that initial scene as a snapshot rather than a movie. Then I asked her to imagine floating up and behind the chair in which she was sitting in the kitchen. With a little effort, she was able to "see" the top and back of her head, me to her right, Tom to her left, and the snapshot of herself in the car ready to drive to work. I helped Carol to maintain this dissociated (detached) position by lowering my tone of voice and by having Tom maintain a light touch on her left arm as soon as she "saw" herself seated in the chair. The touch is simply a stimulus to secure or anchor the detached state, much like hearing a specific song can elicit special feelings and bring you back in time. Tom's touch and my tone of voice helped her to maintain this detached state.

At this point, I asked Carol to "remain safely back here behind Carol in the chair and watch as Carol in the chair watches that scene way over there in the past as the younger Carol drives to work." This weird language also helped her to maintain distance from the memory so that she could remain calm and secure while watching the events of the accident unfold.

I continued to talk in this way, assisting Carol in watching the event of the accident. She said that she was able to recall the moment of impact, her screams, and the thought that she was going to die. According to my understanding of neuroscience, it is unlikely that she could actually recall the moment of impact, since the memory of the collision did not have time to enter long-term memory. Perhaps Carol merely imagined recalling the moment of impact. But on the other hand, maybe just about everything that happens to us is stored in memory and Carol's recall could have been accurate.

As soon as this memory occurred to her, she opened her eyes and tears streamed down her cheeks. I asked Tom to increase the pressure of the touch on Carol's left arm and directed her to "continue to remain back here and watch Carol watch Carol way over there in the past in that accident. And stay securely here as we watch the younger Carol way over there in the past."

It was clear that Carol was feeling calm and secure. She said in a soft voice that she could see everything that was happening. Finally she said that the accident was over and she could see Carol unconscious in her car. Then I asked her to go to Carol in the car and assure her that she survived and that everything would be okay. I asked her to make sure that Carol understood and felt secure in this knowledge. In a few moments, she nodded and said, "She understands." Then I asked Tom to release the anchor (his hand on her arm) and had Carol return to present time in the kitchen.

Carol looked relaxed but a bit puzzled. "I remembered hitting the windshield. Why? Why couldn't I remember it before?"

I said that I didn't know for sure, but probably the memory was there all along at a subconscious level and that's what was causing her fear of driving. Then I asked her to think about the accident and driving and see how she felt. She said that she felt fine, that it wasn't upsetting for her now. I asked her if she thought she could drive.

She said she felt that she could, so I told her to go ahead.

"Now?" she asked.

"Yes, now. The only way you'll know for sure that the fear is gone is if you are able to drive comfortably."

So Carol got her keys, went outside, and drove away in her car. She was gone for about ten minutes and returned to tell us that she did fine. She didn't have the least bit of anxiety. She said that when she came to a stop sign on her drive, the memory of the impact was vivid in her mind and she questioned again as to why that happened. I asked her if it was upsetting for her and she indicated that it wasn't upsetting, just puzzling.

This treatment took about forty-five minutes to complete. Carol returned to work shortly after that treatment. Her phobia and the trauma were cured.

A Visual-Kinesthetic Dissociation Technique

As we saw in Carol's case, V/KD helps you to distance yourself from negative emotions while reviewing a traumatic memory or any negative emotion–inducing situation by creating an altered state, very much like a hypnotic state. While the assistance of a trained professional is usually needed to do this technique properly and to avoid severe emotional reactions, one approach to V/KD is the following:

1. Seated in a chair, visualize a snapshot of a moment immediately prior to the traumatic event when you were feeling safe or not experiencing anything in particular.

2. Visualize a snapshot of yourself "over there" in that past, just before the traumatic event occurred.

3. Next, create the experience of floating up and behind your body in the chair. Now you are looking at yourself in the chair, looking at the snapshot of the younger you way over there in the past about to go through that traumatic event.

4. As soon as you achieve the detached state, hold the thumb, index, and middle fingers of one hand together. This creates a stimulus or anchor that holds the state in place.

5. While maintaining this detached state, allow the "movie" of the event to unfold from beginning to end. It might be necessary to view the movie more than once in this way to be certain that any painful emotion connected with the event is eliminated.

6. After you have reviewed the entire event, become aware of any understandings needed in order to support resolution. For instance, it may become evident that it is over and you survived, that you have learned something of value, or that you now have something of importance to offer others who have been through similar events.

7. In imagery and internal dialogue, share this knowledge and understanding with your "past self," the one who suffered the trauma. Float over to the younger self and share this knowledge until you see that the younger you is able to understand and appreciate this knowledge.

8. Once your "younger self" is feeling safe and secure, "reach out and take hold" of the younger self and "bring you into yourself" so that you may feel forever safe.

Eye Movement Desensitization and Reprocessing (EMDR)

Since Francine Shapiro developed EMDR in 1987, considerable research has been conducted that supports this approach as a highly effective treatment for trauma-related conditions (Shapiro 1995). As an EMDR therapist guides you, you review a traumatic memory while moving your eyes bilaterally. At the same time, you attend to emotional and physical sensations associated with the traumatic memory. Subjective units of discomfort (SUD) in the range of 0 to 10 are monitored throughout the process, and the therapist guides you through sets of eye movements as relevant aspects of the memory emerge. After a significant reduction in discomfort with the memory (usually aiming for a SUD of 0), you rehearse in your mind a relevant positive phrase, such as "I'm safe and I survived," while doing additional sets of eye movements. This phrase helps to replace unhealthy thoughts, such as "I'm damaged forever." During EMDR, associated memories often come to mind and are treated similarly with eye movements. EMDR also includes a "body scan" to evaluate progress and determine targets for additional sets of eye movements. During the closure phase, the therapist offers debriefing suggestions, including relaxation exercises to practice between sessions. In addition to eye movements, EMDR can be done through bilateral sounds, light, and physical tapping. When using sound, the therapist can simply snap his or her fingers alternately near each ear. One method of using light involves a device that alternately flashes light in each eye. EMDR was particularly helpful in treating my client Sandi.

■ Sandi's Story

Sandi was one of the most shy, socially phobic people I ever met. Even after fifteen therapy sessions, she could still hardly look into my eyes and it was difficult to get her to say much. Talk about pulling teeth! Eye movement desensitization and reprocessing (EMDR) to the rescue! I figured this would at least give us something to do during the session.

I asked Sandi if she would like to feel more comfortable in our sessions and with other people. I noticed a subtle nod.

"I take it that's a yes?" I inquired.

She nodded again and this time she was able to say yes in her hardly perceptible soft voice.

I explained that I had recently studied EMDR, which involves focusing on a trauma or a symptom while moving your eyes back and forth. Among a few other things, I then asked her to observe where she felt the shyness and anxiety in her body, and to rate the discomfort level from 0 to 10. At this point, I asked her to pay attention to the feelings while she followed my hand as I moved it back and forth in front of her eyes.

After twenty or so sweeps, she indicated that there was no change. After several sets like this, she still observed no change.

"Oh, well. That's not doing anything," I thought. So I told her that sometimes this process results in something happening between sessions, such as a recall of important memories connected to the symptom. I said that I seriously doubted that this would happen, but I still taught her some things she could do if she became upset later on.

A couple days later, Sandi called me and inquired if the "eye movement technique" could have made her recall something from her past. I said that was possible and that I had mentioned this to her after the EMDR session. She said that she recalled something upsetting and that she would like to have another session sooner to discuss this memory with me and to hopefully feel better. I scheduled her for the next day.

Sandi recalled a series of events from her childhood that were embarrassing and humiliating. Whenever Sandi did not move her bowels for a couple days, her mother would become concerned and insist on giving her an enema. Whenever Sandi put up a fuss, her mother would call whoever was in the house at the time (siblings, aunts, uncles, and neighbors) to chide her until she consented. This was so traumatic for Sandi that she repressed the painful memories.

Initially, recalling the enema incidents was highly upsetting for her. So *we did some more sets of eye movements combined with another technique. This alleviated Sandi's trauma, shyness, and anxiety. She became the outgoing and confident person that she was before suffering the humiliation.*

How and why EMDR works is still being discussed. One hypothesis is that bilateral stimulation jump-starts a self-healing information-processing mechanism in the brain. Dual focus of attention to both the present situation (the therapy situation that includes eye movements) and to the traumatic event (for Sandi, her humiliating childhood experience) makes it easier to observe rather than relive the event. EMDR may also create a relaxation response, which competes with the anxiety and other negative emotions of the trauma. This is another example of Wolpe's reciprocal inhibition (that is, you can't be relaxed and anxious at the same time). Additionally, the eye movements likely send electrical charges (neuronal bursts) that affect the synapses involved in the traumatic memory and this causes a change in how the memory is experienced. EMDR appears to process the traumatic event to an adaptive resolution, although it can result in considerable emotional upset similar to that which frequently occurs with other forms of exposure therapy. Therefore the assistance of a skilled EMDR therapist is important.

While EMDR is the most popular and most extensively researched approach that uses eye movements to treat trauma and many other psychological problems, there are at least three similar approaches that also use eye movements: rapid eye technology (Johnson 1994), eye movement integration (EMI) (Andreas and Andreas 1995), and one eye techniques (Cook and Bradshaw 1999).

Thought Field Therapy (TFT)

Roger J. Callahan began to develop *thought field therapy* in 1979, initially calling it the Callahan Techniques (Callahan 1985). When treating trauma, TFT involves attuning to or thinking about the traumatic memory while physically tapping on specific acupuncture meridian points in sequence. The therapist often uses a diagnostic process with manual muscle testing to determine the necessary treatment points. However, certain sequences of treatment points (algorithms) are found to be effective for different kinds of psychological problems. TFT is based on the idea that psychological problems are the result of energetic information in thought fields. A thought field has a physical reality in the same way that electromagnetic and gravitational fields exist. TFT helped me treat my client Chuck, who suffered from PTSD.

■ Chuck's Story

Chuck was a muscular man with a large frame, 6 feet tall and 250 pounds. During the Vietnam War, he was in the Marines when he suffered a horrific trauma. He was on an aircraft carrier and a jet coming in for a tailhook landing snapped the cable, which went flying like a whip in all directions, hitting several men and amputating body parts. The jet crashed into the deck, and Chuck was involved in putting out the fire and aiding the many injured. That happened over twenty years before he came to see me, and he was still experiencing recurrent nightmares and flashbacks, generalized anxiety, and other PTSD symptoms.

After discussing the possible benefits of treating this trauma by having him physically tap on specific acupuncture meridian points, he agreed to give it a try. I took him through a trauma algorithm, or sequence, that involved him tapping with his fingertips at the following acupoints: beginning of an eyebrow (on the bladder meridian), under an eye (stomach meridian), six inches under an armpit (spleen/pancreas meridian), and under the collarbone next to the sternum (kidney meridian). We did many rounds of this sequence combined with related techniques. Initially the distress level was a 10, and we proceeded to peel away the layers of the trauma. Within twenty minutes, Chuck was able to mentally review the event in detail without experiencing any distress. The SUD was now 0! A follow-up visit two weeks later found that he was no longer having nightmares or flashbacks about this event. While he had experienced other war traumas that required additional treatment, resolution of those events proceeded successfully in a similar manner and he was freed of PTSD.

A Thought Field Therapy Sequence

A standard TFT trauma algorithm, or sequence, involves the following steps (see diagram 1 in chapter 4 for the location of these meridian points):

1. Think about the traumatic memory.

2. Rate the SUD level 0 to 10, with 10 being the highest level of discomfort.

3. Tap with your fingers on each of the following meridian points in sequence: beginning of an eyebrow above the bridge of the nose (bladder meridian), directly under an eye orbit (stomach meridian), six inches under an armpit (spleen/pancreas meridian), and under the collarbone next to the sternum

(kidney meridian). After tapping these points, the SUD generally drops by several points.

4. Next you do the nine gamut treatments. This involves tapping between the little and ring fingers on the back of a hand (triple warmer meridian) while doing the following: eyes closed, eyes opened, eyes down left, eyes down right, eyes in a clockwise direction, eyes in a counterclockwise direction, humming a tune, counting to five, and humming again.

5. At this point, the SUD is generally lower and you repeat the tapping sequence: eyebrow, under eye, under arm, and under collarbone. Frequently at this point all or most distress associated with the memory is removed. Repeating these treatments a few times will often eliminate all of the distress.

6. Sometimes it is helpful to add a simple stress buster—the floor-to-ceiling eye roll—when the SUD is in the 0 to 2 range. This involves tapping between the little and ring fingers on the back of a hand (triple warmer meridian) while slowly moving your eyes from the floor to the ceiling.

Similar to the other methods discussed in this chapter, related traumatic memories often emerge when you treat a specific traumatic memory with TFT. You then use the meridian treatments with the new material, which is usually neutralized just as quickly and effectively as the target memory.

Another TFT concept is *psychological reversal* (PR). It is proposed that PR is a reversed energy flow in the meridians that results in a negativistic, self-sabotaging state. When PR is present, the trauma algorithm will not decrease the SUD. PR can be corrected by tapping on the little finger side of your hand (the third acupoint on the small intestine meridian—see diagram 1, chapter 4) while stating several times, "I accept myself even though I have this problem." After PR is corrected, the meridian treatments will work.

Why Do These Techniques Work?

There are many elements that account for the power of these techniques. Let's look at a few of them.

Exposure

You must bring the traumatic memory to mind, which is an important aspect of eliminating the emotional distress. It is essential to put the trauma "online" in order to treat it. To avoid thinking about the event prevents it from being resolved. Some degree of exposure is a feature common to all of these approaches.

Choice

At the same time, voluntary choice is involved. You choose to think about the event, which is very different from the memory being triggered involuntarily. This choosing creates a self-efficacy that is also curative. Being in charge is a lot different than being at the mercy of the distressing memory.

Position of Observer

Rather than simply experiencing the event as if it's happening all over again, you maintain the position of observer throughout the process. Such a shift in perspective helps you to reduce the negative emotion and therefore you find it easier to learn from the experience.

Present Time

With trauma, you tend to lose contact with the present and to experience the past event as if it is happening all over again. That's what is involved with flashbacks. When you primarily focus on what's happening in your immediate environment while thinking about the traumatic memory, this significantly reduces the emotional intensity of the memory. These techniques help you to remain in the present. For example, it's difficult to get caught up in the memory while you are busy tapping at different locations on your body.

Comfort

In chapter 2, we discussed reciprocal inhibition, which means that you cannot experience relaxation and anxiety at the same time. The calmness induced by these techniques competes with the fear and other negative emotions. Comfort, which is what these techniques create, significantly reduces the distress associated with a traumatic memory. Collectively we might call these techniques rapid reciprocal inhibition or rapid desensitization. Since comfort is introduced while you are exposed to the memory, in the future little or no distress will be associated with the memory.

Belief

Obviously if you believe in a technique, you also expect it to work. While in some instances a technique may work even if you don't believe in it, believing is a definite plus. It has also been found that the effectiveness of medication and surgery is increased as a result of your belief, what is called the *placebo effect*. And the power of belief is such that belief itself is sometimes sufficient to help you overcome a problem.

Pattern Interruption and Restructuring

Each of these techniques also causes a significant change in the way you remember the event. For example, prior to tapping you recalled the event without the stimulation of tapping. After the tapping, the memory is disrupted and no longer stored in your nervous system in the same way it was previously stored (or, for that matter, it may no longer be stored at all). The memory is altered or overwritten. Therefore your new memory of the event does not include negative emotions. Activation of the amygdala—the part of the brain that causes many negative emotions, including fear—does not occur with this new memory. The structure or pattern of the trauma in your energy and nervous systems is interrupted and then restructured.

Bioenergy

Ongoing trauma can be accounted for by brain structures, neurochemistry, memories, and electrical impulses. When you have ongoing psychological trauma, millions of neurons and synapses are also activated, which involves electrical current. Additionally, electrical current always includes electromagnetic fields. These fields involve electromagnetic information stored in your body similarly to the way music, movies, and photos are stored in a computer hard drive or MP3 player. Similar to the way the information in these files can be erased by using a strong electromagnetic field, trauma stored in our nervous system can be altered or erased. Essentially this alteration or erasure is a manifestation of physics or, more precisely, neurophysics.

Now that we've explored some of the complementary and alternative treatments for trauma and PTSD, we're ready to turn our attention in the next chapter to the promising new field of energy psychology (EP).

4

The New Energy Psychology

$E = mc^2$

Matter and energy are both but different manifestations of the same thing.

—Albert Einstein

Revolutionary discoveries were made in the field of physics during the first two decades of the twentieth century. In 1905, Albert Einstein discovered that matter and energy are equivalent. His famous equation, $E = mc^2$, is a summary of that finding. Shortly after, Niels Bohr, Max Planck, and other physicists advanced our understanding of atoms, subatomic particles, and energy. Essentially everything is made of the same stuff, and this also seems to apply to our minds. While Einstein concluded that "matter and energy are both different manifestations of the same thing," in the view of energy psychology, matter, mind, and energy are all different manifestations of the same thing.

Two principal findings of energy psychology (EP) are these:

1. When you have a psychological problem, there is a disruption in your body's energy system.

2. Techniques that return your body's energy system to balance will eliminate the problem.

While psychological problems such as trauma and PTSD can involve numerous contributing factors—for example, heredity; developmental history; activity of the brain, heart, and glands; environmental triggers; thoughts; beliefs; and biochemistry—the most basic contributors are your own body's energy and energy fields. Eliminating problems at this level is the most thorough avenue toward healing.

What Is This Energy?

Physicists define energy as the capacity or power for work. Everything is and operates as a result of energy in its different forms. Think of a rock falling off a cliff and hitting the ground. It's easy to see the energy involved in the fall, but that rock also had potential energy when it sat on the cliff. Then, interaction with the earth's gravitational field produced kinetic energy, or movement, and the rock crashed to the ground. In a similar way, the sun emits light and heat, energy that is absorbed by plants that in turn convert this energy (photosynthesis) to grow and produce oxygen. Food is potential energy that you consume to do work in your body, including moving muscles, producing cells, fighting disease, and even thinking and feeling. To produce these results, the food you eat is converted into chemical and electrical energy. You couldn't be or do anything without energy.

Energy and Ancient History

We've inherited a long and rich history of ideas concerning energy and its relevance to us. About seven thousand years ago in India and other parts of Asia, the universe and human beings were considered to be concrete expressions of divine spiritual energy or *prana* (Sanskrit, to breathe), a life force that pulsates throughout the universe. (Similarly, in the Judeo-Christian tradition, humans are said to be made in the "image" of God and, at creation, God breathed life into the first human.) In the Indian subcontinent and other parts of Asia, this belief held that the body's energy system included the "aura," "chakras," and "marma points" (see below). The physical body and other material objects were seen as the visible condensation or compression of this energy. We might call this understanding of the human and material world a "bioenergy system." Although there is no compelling scientific evidence for the existence of prana, auras, or chakras, modern physics and technology confirm that everything is composed of energy and energy fields. Even subatomic particles such as electrons and quarks are not really particles at all, but pulsating energy.

Aura

According to tradition, the outermost aspect of your body's energy system is the *aura field*. This field surrounds your body in seven layers, with each purported to have specific significance. For example, the layer closest to the physical body is called the "etheric body" and reportedly reflects issues such as self-acceptance and self-love. The seventh and outermost layer is the "spiritual body," which entails serenity and your ability to understand greater universal patterns.

While these ancient notions, as we said earlier, have not been proved scientifically, some people claim that they can actually see auras. Maybe this was the case with artists who painted pictures of holy people with halos around their heads. One method that is reported to help you develop the ability to see auras is to defocus your eyes and maximize your peripheral vision while looking at people and objects. This is similar to what happens when you are in deep reverie or trance. For example, about thirty years ago, I was listening to a hypnotist telling a story to another person about a famous hypnotist who told stories to induce trance and make therapeutic suggestions. After listening to him for several minutes, I suddenly saw a multicolored aura around his head and upper body that persisted for several minutes. While I'd like to believe that I have higher sensory acuity and that I was not simply in a trance at the time with my eyes defocused, it is also possible that my vision was the result of his hypnotic suggestion outside of my awareness.

Nevertheless, there is evidence that electromagnetic fields emanate from your body. Studies have measured the field from the heart as five thousand times stronger than the field from the brain, reaching distances eight to ten feet away (Childre and Martin 1999). Also, Harold Saxon Burr (1972) and his associates at Yale University measured electrical current and electromagnetic fields, what he called "fields of life" or "L-fields," in and around animals, plants, and humans. He suggested that L-fields account for the stable material form of all living things in the same way that an electromagnetic field arranges iron filings in a specific form. Isn't it interesting that your body—your stable form—is essentially the same today as it was four years ago even though every cell and atom is replaced about every four years?

Chakra

Another aspect of this ancient bioenergy system is the *chakra* [Sanskrit *cakram*, wheel, disk, or vortex). Just as there are seven aura layers, there are seven primary chakras. Lucky seven, I guess! They correlate with major nerve ganglia from the spinal column and also relate to levels of consciousness, developmental issues, colors, sounds, and more. For example, the first is the root chakra, which is located at the base of your spine and is related to issues of survival, security, and self-esteem. The seventh is the crown chakra, which is located at the top of your head and pertains to intuitive knowing and spirituality. While these specific notions have not been scientifically proved either, some people claim that they can actually see chakras extending from the body. Try placing the palm of a hand at various distances from the top of your or a friend's head, forehead, throat, and heart. Can you feel the differences in radiant heat? These are electromagnetic fields. Could this be evidence for chakras? There are various therapeutic approaches that emphasize restoring balance to auras and chakras as ways of treating physical and psychological problems (Gallo 2002).

Marma Points

Another aspect of this system is "marma points" (Sanskrit *mru* or *marr*, junction), which are small pockets of prana energy in your body. According to Ayurvedic medicine, any injury to these points not only can be painful and cripple the local functions but can even lead to sudden death. Massaging marma points is one of the many methods used in Ayurvedic medicine to restore your health. To some extent, these marma points correlate with the acupoints used in acupuncture.

Energy Passage

This tradition also holds that energy comes into your body through the aura and the chakras. The chakras are energy transducers (converting energy from one form to another, like plant photosynthesis). When your aura and chakra systems are in balance, there is a harmonious flow of energy and you are emotionally and physically healthy. When you are emotionally disturbed or physically ill, the systems are not in balance and the flow of energy is disrupted.

Meridians

These beliefs about prana developed into methods of dealing with body energies, including yoga, massage, diet, herbs, and more. Then about five thousand years ago, some people in China took up these ideas and developed acupuncture and "moxibustion" (burning a cone of cotton, wool, or other combustible material on or near the skin to produce analgesia or to treat diseases). These therapeutic techniques are based on the idea that your body's energy system also follows pathways called *meridians*. The meridian system includes twelve bilateral (two-sided) primary meridians that are associated with specific organs such as the lungs, heart, stomach, large intestine, and liver. There are also two collector vessels that divide the two sides of your body on the front (central vessel) and back (governing vessel) as well as a number of lesser known vessels that connect with the twelve primary meridians. The energy of the meridian system, referred to as *qi* in the Chinese system (pronounced chee, as in cheese, and often written ch'i), circulates throughout your body. Qi is equivalent to prana. In a sense, there is only one meridian because all are interconnected. Interestingly, qi is not only translated as energy but also as influence, power, and mind. Remember modern physics defines energy as the capacity (or power) for work. The ancient system, however, also maintained the notion that this force is intelligent.

But Do Qi and Meridians Exist?

While not everyone agrees that qi and meridians exist, in the 1970s researchers discovered that there is lower electrical resistance at many acupoints and that, unlike the skin around them, they conduct electrical current. This suggests that meridians and acupoints are real and electrical (Reichmanis, Marino, and Becker 1975). Also, in the 1980s, researchers in France injected a radioactive isotope (technetium) into specific meridian acupoints on 330 patients and observed that the isotopes traveled the meridian pathway (de Vernejoul, Albarede, and Darras 1985). Additionally, it should be noted that acupuncture is regularly used to effectively treat many medical problems such as pain and addiction. This and other lines of evidence offer support for a bodily energy system that follows the ancient meridian maps and has electromagnetic qualities, including light, sound, and subtle electrical current.

Bioenergy

Even if meridians, chakras, and auras are just a mystical fantasy of an ancient civilization, modern physics has established that your body is still made of energy and operates via energy. The nervous system and the body as a whole function as a result of electrochemical impulses. Chemistry is involved, but more fundamentally it is energy in the form of electricity that accounts for the activity of your internal organs, your movements, emotions, and even thoughts. Your brain cells (neurons) carry detailed information through interconnecting synapses. Within each synapse, chemicals assist the flow of electrical impulses, called "action potential," to and away from neurons. Electrical impulses travel to the "soma" or neuron body through extensions called "dendrites" and electrical impulses travel away from the cell body through extensions called "axons."

But your internal communication network is not limited to the nervous system. Research conducted by German biophysicist Fritz-Albert Popp and his associates shows that your cells also emit and apparently communicate via light (photons), what he calls "biophotons" (Popp and Beloussov 2003). Interestingly and understandably, the frequencies of light emitted by healthy cells are different from diseased cells. It is common knowledge that light carries an enormous amount of information, as is the case with fiber optics, so you can imagine the trillions of messages sent every second within your internal "fiber optic" network. In a related sense, French biologist Jacques Benveniste discovered that molecules and cells emit specific audio frequency (Benveniste, Aïssa, and Guillonnet 1998). So your cells are talking up a storm: an ongoing audiovisual conference call.

Needles and More

While acupuncture stimulates acupoints with needles, many other methods for stimulating acupoints and the meridian system also exist. Some of these techniques include finger pressure or acupressure, pressure with various devises, rubbing, running your hands in the direction that the energy flows, vacuum on the points with suction cups, electricity, cold laser, and burning moxa on acupoints. Moxa is an herb (mugwort) that is used instead of needles to stimulate acupoints. (See Meridians section above.) The ultimate purpose of these techniques is to treat health problems by getting your qi moving. It is assumed that health problems are the result of stagnant (blocked) or too much qi. Needling and other methods of acupoint stimulation are intended to balance your body's energy system.

Contemporary Origins of Energy Psychology

The recent history of EP began in the mid-1960s when chiropractor George Goodheart pioneered the development of *applied kinesiology* (AK). While AK involves manual muscle testing and many other procedures for holistically diagnosing and treating physical problems, one of the treatment techniques involves holding or tapping on acupoints to improve muscle functioning and relieve pain. Goodheart also explored the benefit of holding certain areas on the head, called neurovascular reflexes, to treat emotional issues. (You'll have opportunities to learn about and practice these techniques in the following chapter.)

Goodheart worked closely with a number of colleagues while developing AK. In 1974, chiropractor John Thie recommended that Goodheart establish the International College of Applied Kinesiology (ICAK) to standardize curricula and establish certification. However, the ICAK was intended for the professional and Thie wanted to see AK techniques available to a wider audience. He then developed *touch for health* (TFH), which is a synthesis of early AK material. Thie's vision was to make it possible for others without medical training to use AK methods to enhance self-health and the health of family members. While the general public has been receptive to TFH, many professionals have also taken this training.

After Goodheart's findings, a number of professionals used AK to treat psychological problems. Psychiatrist John Diamond (1985) investigated affirmations, which he found effective for balancing meridians and treating emotional issues. For example, he reported that guilt feelings associated with the large intestine meridian can often be alleviated with the affirmation "I am basically clean and good." A heart meridian imbalance, which may involve feelings of anger, may be corrected by an affirmation such as "I have forgiveness in my heart." He also explored the health benefits of music, art, posture, and physically thumping on the sternum over the thymus gland (the "thymus thump"). Diamond's method is called *behavioral kinesiology* (BK).

Psychologist Roger Callahan (1985) explored tapping on specific acupoints to treat psychological problems such as phobias, anxiety, and trauma. His thought field therapy (TFT) was discussed in chapter 3 and is among the approaches that most significantly inspired the advancement of EP.

Over the past sixteen years or so, several mental health professionals have developed methods based on similar findings to treat psychological problems (Gallo 2002, 2005). In 1992, I began to study and practice early versions of EP and then began teaching these methods internationally, eventually developing my own approaches that advance EP as an integrative method. Essentially all EP approaches require you to bring a disturbing emotional issue to mind while you stimulate various bodily areas, such as acupoints, chakras, auras, or similar locations. Some of these EP approaches, such as those you will learn in this book, are very simple and suited for self-treatment. Other EP approaches are more complex and are used by therapists to tailor treatment to help you with problems that are not suitable to self-treatment (Gallo 2000, 2002).

Research

Extensive clinical experience as well as field and experimental studies offer compelling evidence that EP works and that the effects last. The current research is covered in great detail in appendix B of this book. One study, however, is worth noting here.

The most extensive preliminary clinical study on the effectiveness of EP was conducted in South America over fourteen years with 31,400 patients (Andrade and Feinstein 2004). A substudy of this group took place over five and a half years with 5,000 patients diagnosed with PTSD and many other psychological disorders. Included in the substudy were only those conditions in which EP and a control group (cognitive behavioral therapy [CBT] plus medication when indicated) could be used.

At the end of treatment and at follow-up periods of one month, three months, six months, and twelve months, the patients were interviewed by telephone by interviewers who had not been involved in the patients' treatment. These follow-up interviews revealed that with CBT/medication, 63 percent of the patients reported some improvement and 51 percent had complete elimination of symptoms. However, with EP alone, 90 percent of the patients reported some improvement and 76 percent had a complete elimination of symptoms. These results are highly significant, indicating that EP was superior to CBT/medication for a wide range of psychological disorders. Furthermore, the average number of sessions in the EP group was three while the average number of sessions in the CBT/medication group was fifteen.

Energy Psychology Basics

Before covering specific ways to eliminate trauma and PTSD, let's explore the basic elements used in energy psychology (EP) and energy tapping (ET). These will provide you with a solid foundation for self-treatment and/or for working successfully with a qualified therapist.

Tuning In

In order to treat any problem with EP techniques, it is important to attune to or "tune in" the problem. Essentially this means bringing the issue to mind or thinking about it. For example, if you had an argument with a friend that still bothers you, the first step in resolving your discomfort is to think about the argument and get in touch with your emotional discomfort about the argument.

So to learn this facet of the method, very briefly bring to mind something that bothers you. Be very specific about it. And, again, just do this briefly. Don't get all wrapped up in the issue. Also, it's not enough to think "my life," but rather think about a specific thing that is happening or has happened in your life. Your life as a whole contains many parts or aspects. I'm certain that there are many positive things to think about, but for the moment your task is to find something negative, something that bothers you. This may be fear of losing your job, worry about your son or daughter, a financial problem, a specific event that happened long ago, or even fear of spiders. Write down this issue. Again, be very, very specific. The more specific the better! The more general you are in describing a problem, the more likely it is that many aspects are involved. The more aspects involved, the more you may need to treat individual aspects before you no longer feel discomfort about the overall issue. It is okay to have a general problem in mind, but for the purposes of this technique, you must find a very specific issue.

Parts of a Whole

When you treat a trauma with EP, it's important to understand that the original traumatic event usually involved many moments in time. The memory of the event comprises many parts or scenes. Each of these can have a different emotional charge and a distinct emotion, such as anger, guilt, shame, jealousy, or sadness. In order for you to experience thorough and ongoing relief, it is necessary to treat all of these, although treating the most significant ones is often sufficient. The scenes of the trauma are interconnected in such a way that resolving the most significant or representative ones will often resolve the others as well. The important thing to remember is that you need to keep treating until the trauma is eliminated: this means that the memory of the event has little or no emotional charge connected to it. It's kind of like a cafeteria tray dispenser. With each one you remove, another pops up until you are out of trays. Your goal is to remove every tray down to the very last. Each part of the trauma carries an emotional charge with it and your job is to treat them all until no emotional charge remains. When you treat a trauma, it is not necessary to relive the event. Simply think briefly about it, rate the SUD (subjective units of discomfort), and then do the tapping or other recommended techniques. From time to time, check your SUD again to determine your level of progress.

Scaling

Now that you have a problem or aspect in mind, it's time to rate the level of discomfort that you feel when you think about it. Rate the level of discomfort on a scale of 0 to 10, with 0 indicating no discomfort and 10 representing maximum discomfort. The purpose of the rating is to make sure you have the problem tuned in and also that you are able to determine if progress is occurring as you do the treatments. Again, just think about the issue briefly and rate it from 0 to 10.

This scaling might be referred to by many names, including level of discomfort (LOD), subjective units of upset (SUU), or subjective units of discomfort or distress (SUD). Since it is common in the field to use the SUD term, this is the term that we use in this book.

Some people have a difficult time rating the level of discomfort. If this is the case with you, simply call the rating a 10 at the beginning and then measure from there. That will work just as well. Children may also have a difficult time coming up with a number, so other measurements can work too. For example, a 10 might be called "really, really bad," an 8 could be "really bad," a 6 might be "bad," 0 as "really, really good," and so on. Smiley faces can also be used:

Tapping

Tapping is one way of stimulating specific treatment points on your body so that the SUD associated with the issue lessens. The points to be tapped are covered in detail on the next page. However, at this point you need to understand some of the specifics about tapping itself. Use two fingers, such as your index and middle finger, to tap on the areas of your body indicated. The areas to be tapped are located under your eyes, at the center of your forehead slightly above your eyebrows, under your nose, and at other places on your body. The tapping should be firm but not too hard; it shouldn't hurt. The tapping is done continuously. Sometimes it's better to tap quickly, and other times slower or rhythmically. Notice if the way you are tapping is reducing the SUD. If not, change the way you're tapping. Generally you only have to tap five to ten times at each treatment point before moving on to the next treatment point. Also, there are many treatment points on both sides of the body. Some people prefer to tap on one side as compared to the other, and others prefer to tap on both sides at the same time. You can use the fingers on either hand to do the tapping. This is all a matter of personal preference.

Alternatives to Tapping

If you find the tapping to be irritating, you can substitute a number of alternative methods. One is to simply place your fingers at the various treatment points and apply pressure, or take a deep breath while applying the pressure with your fingertips. Another option is to gently massage the point in a circular motion. Sometimes it is sufficient for you to simply imagine tapping the treatment point, although this technique usually works better after you have previously physically stimulated the treatment points by holding, rubbing, or tapping.

Some other ways to stimulate treatment points and focus your attention include patting or holding the palm of your hand at various locations, such as on your forehead, at the back of your head, or at the center of your chest. Some of the techniques covered in this book involve these alternative methods of stimulation.

Tapping Points

With energy tapping, you frequently tap on acupoints to treat the problem. As I mentioned earlier, when you are experiencing a psychological problem, such as a trauma, you also have an energy imbalance or disruption. This shows up in various systems in your body, including the nervous system, glandular system, and meridian system. Although it is not covered in this book, one way to assess which meridians are involved in a problem is by using muscle testing (Gallo 2000). However, you don't need to know how to do muscle testing in order to treat trauma. The techniques covered in this book are usually all that you need.

While there are over 350 acupoints that acupuncturists use to treat varieties of physical problems, you only need a few acupoints to treat trauma. (See diagram 1: Basic Energy Tapping Treatment Points.) Here are descriptions of the locations and abbreviations of the basic meridian acupoints used in this book:

Third Eye (TE): Between and slightly above nose on forehead (Governing Vessel-24.5)

Eyebrow (EB): Beginning of eyebrow at bridge of nose (Bladder-2)

Under Eye (UE): On the bony orbit under the eye (Stomach-1)

Under Nose (UN): Above upper lip and under nose (Governing-26)

Under Bottom Lip (UBL): depression between lower lip and chin (Central-24)

Under Collarbone (UCB): next to sternum under the collarbone (Kidney-27)

Chest (CH): below center of throat on upper section of chest bone (Central-20)

Under Arm (UA): six inches under the armpit (Spleen-21)

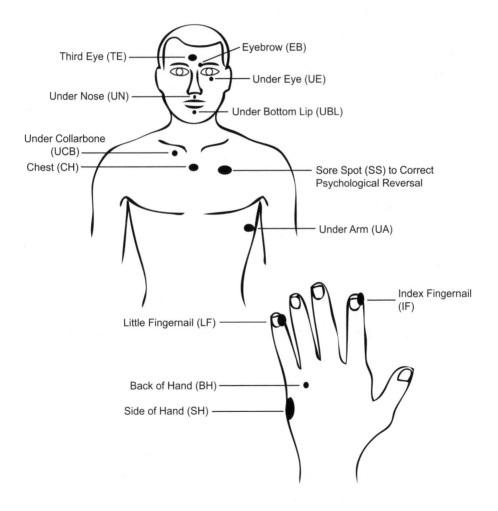

Diagram 1: Basic Energy Tapping Treatment Points

Index Fingernail (IF): on the thumb side of the index fingernail (Large Intestine-1)

Little Fingernail (LF): on the little fingernail facing the ring finger (Heart-9)

Side of Hand (SH): on the little-finger side of the hand (Small Intestine-3)

Back of Hand (BH): between little and ring fingers toward wrist on back of hand (Tri-Heater-3)

Brain Balancer (BB)

Frequently after tuning in a problem, rating the SUD, and tapping on specific treatment points, it is helpful to do a brain balancer. Brain balancers activate many areas of your brain, including the right and left hemispheres, visualization areas, internal dialogue areas, and areas that regulate feelings. Brain balancers assure that the tapping, which has decreased stress and instilled a comfortable feeling, resonates or is distributed throughout your brain and other parts of your body and mind. This increases the chances that the problem is being treated more thoroughly and globally. Also, after using a brain balancer, you will often (but not always) experience a decrease in SUD.

Here's a brain balancer that you will use in this book:

Continually tap on the back of your hand between your little finger and ring finger while doing the following:

Close your eyes.

Open your eyes.

Rotate your eyes in a circle clockwise while humming a tune.

Rotate your eyes in a circle counterclockwise while multiplying any series of numbers, such as 12 × 2 = 24, 12 × 3 = 36, etc.

Again, rotate your eyes in a circle clockwise while humming a tune.

Stress Reducers

When your SUD is 0 to 2 after treating trauma or other problems with ET, the floor to ceiling eye roll (ER) or elaborated eye roll (EER) can help to reduce stress further or to "seal in" the treatment results. Try these techniques now.

Floor to Ceiling Eye Roll (ER)

To do the Eye Roll (ER), keep tapping on the back of your hand (BH) while slowly and steadily moving your eyes from the floor to the ceiling. While continuing to tap, hold your eyes in this raised position for a few seconds, stop tapping, and then check your SUD level again. Usually you will feel more relaxed after doing ER.

Elaborated Eye Roll (EER)

The Elaborated Eye Roll (EER) includes a few distinctions that produce even deeper relaxation. To do the EER, keep tapping on the back of the hand (BH) while slowly and steadily moving your eyes from the floor to the ceiling. Then continue to tap and keep your eyes raised while lowering your eyelids and taking a deep breath. (Ideally just the whites of your eyes show at this point in the procedure.) Then quit tapping and exhale while resting your eyes in the closed position. Check your SUD level again. Usually you will feel very relaxed after doing EER.

Switching (Neurologic Disorganization)

Generally when you tap on the treatment points while attuning a specific issue, the SUD starts to decrease fairly quickly and in significant increments. For example, if you start off with a 10, after tapping and using a brain balancer the SUD may drop to 7. After another round of tapping, it may drop to a 5 and then 3 and so on. However, sometimes the SUD will descend very slowly—such as one increment or a fraction of an increment after each round of tapping. Frequently this indicates a condition referred to as *switching*, which may involve a "scrambling" of energy so that you cannot adequately attune to the issue. This can be corrected by doing the following technique:

HOOK-UP TECHNIQUE

1. Sit in a chair, extend your legs in front of you on the floor, and cross your left ankle over your right.

2. Extend your arms in front of you with the backs of your hands touching. Next, raise your right hand over your left so that the palms are touching and interlock your fingers. Lower your arms and then raise them so that your hands now rest on your chest.

3. While holding this position, place your tongue to the roof of your mouth about one-half inch behind your upper teeth.

4. Slowly breathe in through your nose and out through your mouth for approximately one minute.

After doing the Hook-Up Technique, resume tapping. The SUD will then often decrease more efficiently.

Besides correcting switching, the Hook-Up also improves focus and concentration. I have found this technique, used by itself, helpful for some children and adults who experience problems with attention, concentration, and even coordination.

Psychological Reversal

As effective as these techniques are, the SUD sometimes does not decrease regardless of how much you tap, rub, or hold. This can be due to a psychological block known as psychological reversal. (It is sometimes called "psychoenergetic reversal," or simply "reversal.") Basically, psychological reversal is an issue in front of or intertwined with the issue that you are trying to resolve. Although you may say that you want to get over a specific problem, a part of you (a kind of subself) opposes your healthy intention. That part resists cooperating and expresses that resistance through self-sabotage. This is an unfortunate aspect of the human condition, something that we all have to contend with in life. For example, you firmly decide to lose weight or quit doing something that is not good for you, and then you still don't change your behavior. People are known for saying, "Well, then you really don't want to change!" But is this truly the case, or is your energy misaligned and moving in the opposite direction? In many instances, I think this reflects a kind of reversed polarity similar to the way that a motor will turn in the opposite direction if you alter the positive and negative electrical wires attached to it. The techniques in this book show you how to reattach those "wires" so that you are aligned with your best intentions. At other times, psychological reversal may reveal that you have another overriding issue that needs attention before you can address the specific problem (such as excess weight) that you seek to resolve. Frequently reversal can be corrected by doing the Karate-Chopping Exercise below:

KARATE-CHOPPING EXERCISE

Continually tap the little-finger side of your hand (SH) against the palm of your other hand (karate-chopping style), or tap your fists together with clenched fingers facing you. As you do this, say the following several times in a convincing tone:

"Even though I have this problem, I deeply and completely accept myself."

It's helpful to know that you don't have to believe this statement in order for it to work. Also, it is often useful to replace the term "problem" with the specific issue. For example:

"Even though I'm upset with Bob, I deeply and completely accept myself."

OR

"Even though I'm upset about my accident, I deeply and completely accept myself."

You may find it helpful to modify the statement so that it indicates elimination of the problem. For example:

"Even though I have this trauma, I deeply and completely accept myself, and I choose to no longer have this trauma."

OR

"Even though I have this trauma, I deeply and completely accept myself, and I'm willing to no longer have this trauma."

OR

"Even though I'm upset with Bob, I deeply and completely accept myself, and I'm willing to no longer be upset with Bob."

Sometimes the reversal shows up in the form of an issue concerning your ability or the appropriateness of getting over the problem. For example, in some respects you might feel that you don't deserve to get over the problem, or that it's not safe to get over the problem, or that it's impossible to get over the problem, or that you would be violating a sense of loyalty to someone if you got over the problem. These kinds of issues can be treated by using the same basic technique but changing the wording as follows:

"Even if I don't deserve to get over this problem, I deeply and completely accept myself."

"Even if a part of me believes it's impossible for me to get over this trauma, I deeply and completely accept myself, and I'm willing to get over this trauma."

The New Energy Psychology   59

"Even if it isn't safe for me to get over this trauma, I deeply and completely accept myself, and I choose to get over this trauma."

"Even if a part of me believes that I would not be loyal to (person's name) by getting over this problem, I deeply and completely accept myself, and I'm willing to get over this problem."

Sometimes the Karate-Chopping Exercise does not work to correct the reversal. In these cases, other places to tap that may work include the following (see diagram 2: Psychological Reversal Correction Points):

- The sore spot (SS), which is a tender spot on the left side of your chest, between the second and third ribs above the breast

- Under your nose (UN)

- Under your bottom lip (UBL)

- Under your collarbones next to the sternum (UCB)

- Upper portion of the center of your chest (CH)

- Back of your hand between the little and ring fingers (BH)

- Under your eyes (UE) on the bony orbit of the cheekbone

Reversal Is Just Another Problem

Although the affirmations listed above are often used to correct reversals, saying the affirmations is not always necessary. If you find that your SUD is not decreasing while treating a trauma, assume that there is a reversal and simply tap one or several of the psychological reversal correction points (see diagram 2) with the intention of removing the reversal. Then resume the ET treatment for the identified problem.

It's important to know that frequently you can sense your own mixed feelings or ambivalence about resolving the identified problem. You might feel that you can't get over the trauma, or you might feel angry at yourself for having the trauma, or what have you. When you are able to sense an interfering thought, belief, or emotion, simply make that the first order of business, the first problem to resolve. Next, rate the intensity of this issue 0 to 10 (with 10 being the strongest level of intensity), and then tap one or several of the reversal correction points until you notice that the interference has been neutralized.

Challenging Results

After you treat a problem with EP and your SUD is down to 0 or 1, it is usually helpful to challenge the results. When you challenge the results, you attempt to get the discomfort back (that is, to elevate your SUD again). Now that may seem like an odd thing to do, since your goal is to eliminate the emotional discomfort. But if you are able to bring back the discomfort, this means that the problem is not entirely eliminated and more treatment is needed.

Usually when the discomfort recurs, it is not as strong and your SUD does not return to its original level. Most of the time your SUD will be lower. Obviously this means improvement has already occurred. However, the return of discomfort means that either the aspect of the problem that you have been tuning in has not been thoroughly treated or that another aspect is being tuned in. All this means is that there's some more work to do, but don't get discouraged. (You'll learn more about

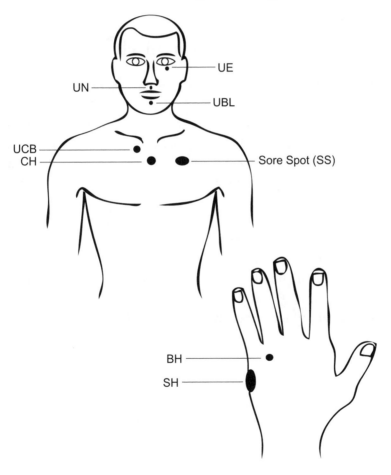

Diagram 2:
Psychological Reversal Correction Points

troubleshooting in chapter 6.) Note the improvement that you've already made and trust that you are well on your way to eliminating the trauma. Generally a few more treatment sessions will completely eliminate the problem.

How Much Should You Tap?

You really don't need to spend a lot of time tapping or doing other EP techniques. The goal is to eliminate the discomfort. Usually it only takes a few minutes to do any of the treatments covered in the next chapter. If you want to treat a few parts or scenes of a trauma or consequences of a trauma (such as a phobic reaction), it's best to spend no more than thirty minutes at one time treating yourself. Then it's good to give yourself a rest and clear your mind of these concerns. There's always tomorrow or perhaps again later in the day.

How Often Should You Treat Yourself?

How often you should treat yourself is an individual matter. Trauma from a single traumatic event can often be effectively eliminated in a few minutes. Of course, this will depend on your level of distress and how well you apply the techniques. Obviously, more complex trauma involving many traumatic events will require more self-treatment over a period of time. However, even the most complex trauma can be effectively treated with these techniques. These issues are covered in detail in the following chapters.

If, after you have treated a trauma, you experience calmness and thoughts about the event do not bother you, there's a good chance that it will not bother you any more. When the treatment works, it is thorough. All of the symptoms associated with the trauma—including flashbacks, intrusive thoughts, bad dreams—are eliminated.

Now that you know EP and ET basics, it's time to focus on how you can clear your traumas and painful memories. Turn with me to chapter 5.

5

How to Use Energy
Tapping for Trauma

We must rid ourselves of yesterday's negative thoughts to receive
today's new and positive feelings.

—Sydney Banks

This chapter will teach you how to use nine EP techniques to treat painful memories, trauma, and the negative results of trauma. All of these techniques access and balance your energy system while eliminating traumatic stress, although not all of them involve physically tapping with your fingers at locations on your body.

Certainly there are some situations, such as the loss of a loved one, which you may not want to resolve completely with EP. Mourning is important. Yet EP can help you move through the grieving process much more comfortably.

Think of this as a workbook chapter. You are invited to actively participate and to experience the techniques, not to simply intellectually learn about them. This is probably just what you've been waiting for, so let's get started.

General Stress-Reduction Techniques

Earlier in this book, we talked about how you can't feel relaxed and anxious at the same time (reciprocal inhibition). Because that is true, stress-reduction techniques can play an important role in treating trauma. By helping you relax, your anxiety lessens and you become more receptive to the healing that is possible through energy tapping. Besides simply feeling good—who can't use a little stress reduction now and then?!—the following techniques lay a healthy and helpful foundation for the ET techniques that we will discuss later in this chapter.

Emotional Stress Release (ESR)

When I was a child, my mother would sometimes hold the front and back of my head with her hands when I was ill. Within moments, I would feel more comfortable. If I felt sick to my stomach and had to vomit, she would hold my head in this way over the sink or commode, and the discomfort of vomiting would ease. For some reason, I felt secure when she did this. Surely this feeling of security and relief was because my mother was helping me in a loving way, but I've also found that this holding technique is often beneficial in itself. Maybe you have also experienced this folk remedy.

You've probably held and even rubbed your forehead when feeling stressed, and seen other people do this too. Somehow the holding and rubbing, if done for a long enough period of time, can significantly reduce the stress. Why is that?

In the early 1990s, I learned about a technique that is equivalent to what my mother did for me and what some people naturally tend to do when stressed. This technique is formally called *emotional stress release* (ESR); an alternative version is frontal/occipital holding (FOH).

In the 1930s, Dr. Terrence Bennett identified many reflexes on the head and some other areas of the body that he referred to as "neurovascular reflexes," also known as the "Bennett reflexes." He believed that these reflexes provide a feedback mechanism to various organs to increase blood flow. By stimulating the reflexes, he concluded, circulation to those organs was improved.

Later Dr. George Goodheart studied these reflexes and correlated them with other findings in applied kinesiology (AK), the field he developed. He also found that the two reflexes on the forehead directly above the eyebrows and on slight protrusions on the forehead, known as the frontal eminences, could be used to treat emotional issues. He called these "emotional neurovascular reflexes." For simplicity, we'll call them "peace points" in the remainder of this section, since you will be able to use them to reduce stress and feel more peaceful.

I have found ESR to be highly effective, both for myself and others, for decreasing stress. I have also demonstrated it hundreds of times at workshops and taught thousands of professionals how to use it; others have found it just as effective as I have. Although ESR works much of the time, some complex traumas require one of the more advanced techniques covered later in this chapter. But ESR is a good place to start for dealing with stress, and it can be an initial step for treating more complex issues. So here is the ESR technique. Rather than simply reading about it, I encourage you to try it right now. Pick a mildly uncomfortable memory and experience the benefits of the technique.

ESR Technique

1. Briefly bring to mind a painful memory or specific scene from that memory.

2. Rate the SUD 0 to 10, with 10 being the highest level of discomfort, or simply call the present level a 10 and measure from there. Or if you prefer, don't even bother with a number if you feel you can sense the stress level decreasing as you move through the technique.

3. Set that memory aside for the time being and place the fingertips of both of your hands on the peace points on your forehead directly above your eyebrows on the slight protrusions on your forehead. (See diagram 3: Emotional Stress Release.) Close your eyes and let your fingers rest there lightly and feel for pulses. They are light, faint pulses and they might be different on each side. If you can't feel the pulses, gently press and move the skin at these locations toward the center and then sides of your forehead. Your thumbs should not be touching the areas, since your thumbs have pulses too and this would make it difficult to sense the pulses from the peace points.

4. Continue to focus on the pulses on each side until they are synchronized, pulsating in unison. If you cannot feel the pulses after some attempts, proceed without taking pulse perception into account.

5. Now think again about that negative memory and notice the discomfort level or rate the SUD. The pulses might not beat at the same rate when you initially bring to mind the memory.

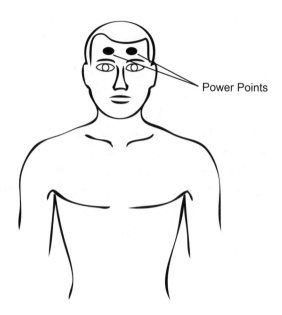

Power Points

Diagram 3: Emotional Stress Release (ESR)

6. Remain focused on the memory and the peace points until the pulses synchronize again. If you can't feel the pulses, simply pay attention to the feeling of your fingertips on your forehead while also keeping the memory in mind.

7. Observe the discomfort level from moment to moment and rate the SUD if you prefer.

8. Usually the issue becomes more difficult to keep in mind as the SUD decreases. When you feel relaxed about the memory, discontinue holding the peace points and relax for about a minute.

9. Next, think about the memory again to determine if there is any remaining stress. If there is, repeat the ESR technique. If there is any remaining stress, it may be related to an aspect of the memory that you were not attuning initially.

10. A few rounds of ESR may be what you need to experience ongoing relief about this memory.

You can also use this ESR technique for any issue related to this memory, such as a phobia or general anxiety as a result of the incident. One businessperson I know used ESR to not only relieve the stress of a legal problem, but also used it to relieve stress about going forward with planned changes in her business. You can also use

ESR as a general stress reducer. Just give yourself a break and hold the peace points when you are feeling stressed. Frequently you will feel better within a few minutes. Adding some deep breathing to the formula can further enhance the effects.

Frontal/Occipital Holding (FOH)

Frontal/occipital holding (FOH) is another version of ESR that you can use to relieve stress in general or for any specific issue, such as a painful memory. It is similar to the basic ESR technique, since the peace points are held while you picture or think about a painful memory, trauma, or other stressful situation. However, with FOH, you place the palm of one hand on your forehead over the peace points and the other palm on the occipital region at the back of the head. This is basically the version that my mother used. FOH tunes in the details of the trauma and helps you to review in a detached manner. While doing FOH, you can also think about the details of the event and begin to alter any negative conclusions or decisions you made at the time. In a sense, you can rewrite history with this technique. Please pick out another mildly to moderately uncomfortable memory and try it now. Here are the steps to follow:

FOH Technique

1. Briefly bring to mind a painful memory or specific scene from that memory.

2. Rate the SUD 0 to 10, or just rate it a 10, or simply notice the tension or emotional intensity you feel so that you'll be able to detect any changes.

3. Now place the palm of one hand on your forehead and the other at the back of your head.

4. Think about that negative memory and continue to observe the stress level from moment to moment. Rate the SUD if you'd like, or simply observe the level of tension or emotional intensity. Usually the issue becomes more difficult to keep in mind as the SUD decreases.

5. When you feel relaxed about the memory, discontinue holding your head and clear your mind for about a minute.

6. Next think about the memory again to determine if there is any remaining stress. If there is, resume FOH. If stress remains, it may be related to an aspect of the memory that you were not attuning initially.

7. A few rounds of FOH may be what you need to experience ongoing relief about this memory.

8. Once you can look at the memory and feel calm about it, notice if you made a decision or drew a conclusion about yourself, life, or something else at the time of the event that you would now like to alter. For example, if you had concluded that you were "damaged," perhaps you would like to make a healthier assessment now, such as that you are strong and you survived. Often becoming calmer about the event will itself help you to change your mind in a healthier direction.

9. To reinforce the healthier decision or conclusion, again do FOH while reviewing the event and holding this healthier belief in mind. Notice as the new belief feels increasingly convincing. You can rate the level of conviction 0 to 10, with 10 now being positive. Aim for the 8 to 10 range.

10. While FOH will help you to experience a significant change in how you feel and think about the event, in some cases it may be necessary to repeat this process a few times before the results last.

ESR and FOH are highly portable techniques that you can use anytime you need to diffuse stress about traumatic scenes, painful memories, or other stressful situations. Like anything, FOH involves a learning curve. The more you practice, the better you get at using the technique and discovering other interesting ways to use it to benefit yourself, family, and friends. But ESR and FOH are just a part of the stress-reduction story. Now let's take a look at the many benefits of breathing.

Alpha-Theta Breathing

Brain waves are measured by an electroencephalograph (EEG), which calculates the waves in tiny oscillating electrical voltages called "hertz" (a few millionths of a volt). The term is in honor of German physicist Heinrich Rudolf Hertz, who made important scientific discoveries about electromagnetism. A hertz is one cycle per second, two hertz is two cycles per second, and so on. The beta brain-wave range is the fastest (although some EEG researchers suggest there is an even faster gamma wave). Beta clips along at 14 to 40 cycles, or hertz, per second, and on a good day is associated with heightened alertness. Alpha range is slower at 8 to 13 hertz, and is associated with relaxed and effortless alertness. Theta is slower yet at 4 to 7 hertz, and involves deeper relaxation, meditation, light sleep, and creativity. And when you are in delta range, you are moving along at 0.5 to 4 hertz, which means that you are deeply asleep.

Slow deep breathing can be very relaxing as it can change the rhythm of your brain waves from high beta to the slower alpha and theta frequencies. Beta waves go together with active awareness, the mental state that you experience when you are active at work and play. Your brain is also in beta when you are analyzing, solving a problem, or confronting threats and emergencies. Stimulants such as caffeine, nicotine, small amounts of alcohol, amphetamines, and even peppermint also can induce beta. Too much beta can result in anxiety, panic, muscle tension, exhaustion, and high blood pressure. If you are experiencing trauma and PTSD, more than likely your brain is chronically beta. Besides the distress of trauma and PTSD, chronic beta also affects your immune system negatively.

Although beta certainly has its benefits, it is important to slow down and relax at times. You know, stop and smell the roses. This is where alpha and theta brain waves come into play. Alpha and theta are states of relaxation and serenity. A good place to aim for is the alpha-theta border, which is a brain-wave range where you have the ability to be at your most serene, creative, intelligent, and peak performing. When you are in this state, you are relaxed and conscious of everything around you, yet protected from stress and in touch with your inner resources. The alpha-theta border is between 7 and 8 hertz. Interestingly, this is essentially the resonant frequency of the earth and the ionosphere—about 7.5 hertz. This is often a good state to be in, and you can get there through meditation, self-hypnosis, and relaxed, deep breathing.

Slow deep breathing also has been found to change brain and blood chemistry and can help you shift from sympathetic nervous system activity to parasympathetic nervous system activity. These are two of the three aspects of the *autonomic nervous system* (ANS) that regulate your heart rate, blood pressure, and various internal organs and glands. When you are in sympathetic mode your nervous system is on alert—ready to fight, run, or maybe even freeze if necessary. Parasympathetic mode is the opposite: relaxed, serene, lower blood pressure, lower heart rate, and so on. It stands to reason that being in a more relaxed parasympathetic mode is healthy, although you actually need a balance between the two. Spending too much time in the sympathetic state can damage you. If you've had a trauma, your nervous system tends to be chronically on alert. When you experienced the traumatic event, your body went on alert, with certain parts of your brain, such as the amygdala, being highly activated—again, sympathetic nervous system activation. The memory of the event, which can be triggered by anything that makes you recall it, puts you back in a state of emergency. We call this a "conditioning effect." But if you bring to mind the event and adjust your breathing to a slower rate, you can diffuse the traumatic stress. It makes good sense to reset your ANS. So give it a try now:

Alpha-Theta Breathing for Trauma

1. Bring to mind the memory of an event that is stressful for you.

2. Rate the SUD level 0 to 10, simply call it 10, or just notice how you feel in your body so you can detect any changes.

3. Set the memory aside for a moment and exhale as much as you can.

4. Now take a slow deep breath up from your diaphragm for the count of ten.

5. Hold your breath for the count of ten without tightening your throat (that is, don't close your glottis, the space between your vocal cords).

6. Now, for the count of ten, slowly exhale (don't rush it) and then force even more air out of your lungs.

7. Breathe normally and think of the memory again. Evaluate your SUD level.

Is it lower now? Is it down to 0? If you have experienced significant progress but are not yet down to 0, repeat the exercise. Repeat it even if you haven't become more relaxed about the event, since several rounds of the exercise are often needed before you shift out of sympathetic mode and enjoy more relaxed brain waves. This time evaluate your stress level by checking in about the memory. As you inhale or exhale, bring the memory to mind and notice how you feel.

Alpha-Theta Breathing for Stress

Alpha-Theta Breathing is also a good way to generally lower your stress level. You don't have to tune in to a stressful event to use it. Simply notice how you feel and then do the breathing cycle twelve times in a row. So don't wait to finish this chapter. Give yourself a healthy breather and do it now:

1. Rate how you feel with 10 being really tense and 0 being amazingly relaxed.

2. Take a slow deep breath up from your diaphragm for the count of ten.

3. Hold your breath for the count of ten without tightening your throat.

4. Now for the count of ten, slowly exhale (don't rush it), and then force even more air out of your lungs.

5. Repeat steps 2 to 4 for an additional eleven times. Don't give in to the urge to inhale or exhale any faster than a normal count of ten.

6. Again rate how you feel.

Alpha-Theta Breathing is a highly portable technique that you can use anytime you need to diffuse stress, including the stress of trauma, painful memories, and other difficult situations. It involves a learning curve, but the more you practice, the better you get. But this technique is also just a part of the story. Now let's take a look at the benefits of energy tapping.

Energy-Tapping Techniques

There are a number of techniques that help you to treat psychological problems by tapping with your fingers on specific acupoints on your body. In this section, you will learn three energy-tapping techniques that are highly effective in eliminating simple and highly complex trauma.

Energy Tapping for Simple Trauma

Simple trauma is any painful event that haunts you and prevents you from moving on with life. It can involve, for example, rejection, a cruel remark, embarrassment, or a mistake for which you continue to punish yourself. (Simple trauma, though distressing, by definition is "simple"; it does not have the magnitude of a traumatic event that results in PTSD.)

This type of trauma, often a single isolated event, can be treated with the technique given later in this section. However, if there is more than one element involved, each scene or event should be treated individually. For example, if the initial event was an insult from your boss that was later followed by an undesirable change in your work schedule, at least two aspects would be involved—the insult and the schedule change—and each would be treated separately.

The first step as always is to tune in or think about the event. It's not necessary to experience discomfort, except briefly when the event is recalled. The purpose of recalling the event is to get a SUD rating and to make sure that the trauma is tuned in and locked in so that it can be successfully treated. To simply do the technique without tuning in something specific might result in a feeling of relaxation, but it would not resolve a specific problem. The memory must be brought into awareness at some level, although the most subtle level is sufficient.

A story from my own life illustrates how energy tapping works for simple trauma. Please note that during treatment, the event is briefly recalled, not focused on.

■ Fred's Story

One cold winter evening, I needed to take my eldest daughter to a school event. Since the driveway was heaped with snow, backing out of the garage was difficult. After a few unsuccessful attempts, I was determined to plow through the snow, so I gunned the accelerator. The car, now out of control, slid suddenly to the left, smashing into the corner of the garage. I pounded the steering wheel and shouted a few choice words as I climbed out of the car to assess the damage. The car had knocked the garage off its foundation, and the garage, in what might be considered an act of self-defense, gouged a long, deep scratch down the side of the car. Still muttering, I grabbed a shovel and attacked the snow with a vengeance, throwing it to the side of the driveway. Finally I was able to drive my daughter to school, but I couldn't shake the events of that evening. I was upset for days. Eventually I realized that perhaps I should practice what I preach, so I tried the simple trauma technique. Within three minutes, I felt calm and peaceful about the crashing encounter with the garage. I could see exactly what had happened that snowy night, but my emotional distress and self-incriminating thoughts were gone. Instead I understood this event as a learning experience and realized that there was really nothing to be accomplished by remaining upset. Ultimately everything would be okay. I also decided that I'd never pull that kind of car stunt again!

Simple Trauma Technique

So let's get down to business again. Bring a simple, painful event to mind and practice the following protocol:

1. Think about the event or specific aspect of the event and rate the discomfort level in any way you prefer (for example, SUD level 0 to 10, with 0 representing no discomfort and 10 representing the highest level of discomfort). This measures how you presently feel as you think about the event, not the way you felt at the time that the event occurred.

2. Correct a possible reversal by tapping continually on the little-finger side of your hand (SH) or rubbing the sore spot (SS) on the left side of your chest while saying or thinking three times, "Even though I'm upset about what happened, I deeply and completely accept myself." You can be specific about the event. (See diagram 4: Energy Tapping for Simple Trauma.)

3. Tap seven to ten times at each of the following meridian points: beginning of one or both eyebrows (EB) near the bridge of your nose, followed by under one or both collarbones next to your sternum (UCB). These points are listed as 1 and 2 on the diagram.

4. Reevaluate how you feel. If the discomfort level has decreased by at least two points, continue; otherwise go to the complex trauma technique later in this chapter.

5. To continue, do the Brain Balancer (BB). Continually tap on the back of your hand (BH) between your little finger and ring finger while doing the following:

Close your eyes.

Open your eyes.

Rotate your eyes in a circle clockwise while humming a tune.

Rotate your eyes in a circle counterclockwise while multiplying any series of numbers, such as 12 × 2 = 24, 12 × 3 = 36, etc.

Again, rotate your eyes in a circle clockwise while humming a tune.

6.   Again evaluate how you feel. After doing the Brain Balancer (BB), your discomfort level will usually decrease, but there are instances where it will remain the same or increase. That's okay. If it increases, this sometimes means that you have tuned in another aspect of the problem. Just continue with the technique.

7.   Again tap seven to ten times at the beginning of one or both eyebrows (EB) near the bridge of your nose, followed by under one or both collarbones next to your sternum (UCB). These points are listed as 1 and 2 on the diagram.

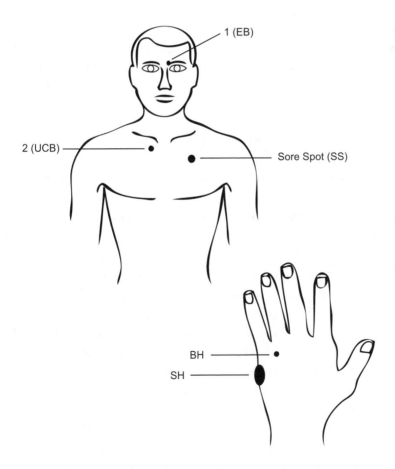

Diagram 4: Energy Tapping for Simple Trauma

8. Again briefly check how you feel. The discomfort level should be even less at this point. If it is, continue to alternate between the two treatment points and the Brain Balancer (BB) until discomfort about the event is gone.

9. If progress comes to a standstill at any point, correct a possible mini-reversal by tapping on the little-finger side of your hand (SH) while saying three times, "Even though I'm still upset about what happened, I deeply and completely accept myself." Then continue alternating between the EB and UCB treatment points and the Brain Balancer (BB).

10. When your discomfort level is within the 0 to 2 range, it is often useful to add the Eye Roll (ER) or Elaborated Eye Roll (EER) one or a few times. For the ER, tap continually between your little finger and ring finger on the back of your hand (BH), slowly raise your eyes from the floor to the ceiling, take a slow deep breath, and then exhale. With the EER, also raise your eyes upward while lowering your eyelids. Check to determine if there is any remaining discomfort.

11. If there isn't any discomfort, see if you can get it back. If you can, it means that there is an aspect that still needs to be treated. Continue with the recipe.

Energy Tapping for Highly Complex Trauma

ET treatment for highly complex trauma works with traumatic or other painful memories that have many aspects and greater complexity in terms of emotional distress. These techniques usually do not change the memories of the traumatic event. Mostly they just eliminate the emotional and physical distress associated with it. So when you have done a trauma treatment successfully, you will feel calm yet still able to recall the event in detail. You may feel, however, somewhat detached from it, and you might notice that you can recall the event more vividly than you could before doing this treatment. This is because you are no longer distracted by emotional upset, making it possible for you to unwaveringly look at and think about what happened. It's as though a memory has different tracks: visual, sound, emotional, and belief. ET erases the negative emotional track but usually not the visual or sound tracks. Since the belief track is generally attached to the emotional track, this track also usually changes in a more positive direction as a result of the treatment.

Some people report that the memory no longer bothers them, and they are no longer able to recall it clearly. The image might be described as vague and way off in the distance. If this happens to you, don't be concerned. You might like, however, to repeat the treatment, since difficulty recalling the event vividly is sometimes an indication that it has not been treated thoroughly. Repetition of the treatment may result in the ability to clearly see and hear what happened in a calm, relaxed manner. Of course, the real proof is when the memory no longer bothers you and all of the symptoms of trauma are gone for good. So not being able to vividly recall the event is not always relevant.

When dealing with highly complex trauma, there are often a number of aspects involved in the traumatic event. Because of this, it is important that each aspect be treated individually. Before describing the technique for doing this, I'd like to share the stories of Barbara and Bill, which illustrate how ET works for people who have experienced highly complex trauma.

■ Barbara's Story: Rape Trauma

Barbara was an attractive thirty-two-year-old married woman who suffered from depression and was dependent on drugs and alcohol. She was admitted to the hospital after taking a large quantity of pills in a suicide attempt, and I was consulted by her physician. She was severely depressed, and during the course of my interview with her, I learned that at age thirteen she was raped by an eighteen-year-old male. They had been drinking at the time. She never told her mother or other family members about the rape, and she developed PTSD with flashbacks, nightmares, depression episodes, dissociation, and pervasive feelings of worthlessness. As is often the case with rape victims, she senselessly blamed herself.

I tried to help Barbara resolve the trauma, since I felt that it was the linchpin that held her depression, chemical dependency, and low self-esteem in place. We had many sessions where I listened to her empathetically and challenged the negative thoughts and limiting beliefs that seemed to be at the core of her misery. I also got her involved in 12-step programs like Alcoholics Anonymous. While she was doing somewhat better, she still limped through life and continued to believe that she was worthless. I, however, felt strongly that she would do much better if the rape trauma was resolved. Yet every time we touched on this issue, she would become extremely upset, crying and degrading herself. So I steered away from the issue, since this was not helping.

After a hiatus of about four months, Barbara returned to therapy. By this time, I had discovered the many benefits of ET and realized as she walked in the door that this might be the solution to her trauma. Initially she came in because she was upset about her mother, so I explained the tapping procedure and treated her in this way. This eliminated the discomfort that she was feeling in the moment, and she was able to think about her mother in more understanding and positive ways. Then I broached the subject of the rape. As soon as we began talking about it, Barbara did what she had always done. She began to cry, shake, and degrade herself. She said that she was to blame, that she never listened to her mother, and that she shouldn't have been out drinking with the boy. Tears streamed down her face. On a scale of 0 to 10, her distress level was at least 15—and I am probably grossly underestimating her pain.

Initially I helped her to calm down by asking her to describe a bronze lamp that sat on an end table in my office. My purpose was to have her focus externally rather than focusing on the internal images of the rape and her emotional distress. After she felt much calmer, I suggested that we do the tapping technique to help her. She agreed. I then asked her to think about the event in detail (something that, after years of using ET, I have found not to be necessary).

While she thought about the event in detail, she again became emotionally upset, but this time I had her use ET. This treatment took less than ten minutes and it completely eliminated the distress of her painful memory. All I had her do was attend to the memory and tap on certain acupoints a number of times. Not only did she no longer experience negative emotion while recalling the event, but her belief about the situation and herself changed in a radically positive direction as well.

Right after the treatment was completed in that incredibly brief time, she was able to tell me with obvious conviction that it was "just something that happened when I was a kid" and that she was "not to blame." This was completely and utterly amazing to me. I also tested the strength of her conviction by reminding her of the self-incriminating and degrading statements that she had made earlier, but her confidence and conviction remained unshaken. She said she knew she had said those things, but now she understood it wasn't true. The meaning of the event was transformed completely and profoundly without attempting to directly challenge her negative thoughts about herself. That is, we didn't have to use cognitive behavioral therapy (CBT) to get this result. And I doubt that CBT could have made it possible to get these kinds of results so quickly.

Don't be mistaken, Barbara was not instantly and completely cured of all her problems as a result of this brief treatment. However, the trauma was absolutely and completely eliminated within a few minutes. In turn, that change made it easier for her to improve in other areas of her life. Over the course of several months, we used other ET treatments to help her control addictive urges and to eliminate depression and anxiety. I did phone call follow-ups with Barbara over the course of ten years and the trauma remained completely resolved. She was able to recall the event in detail; however, it no longer caused her emotional distress. I am also pleased to tell you that after eliminating that trauma, Barbara went to graduate school and eventually became a licensed psychotherapist.

The trauma that Barbara suffered is an example of a complex or highly complex trauma. While I previously divided these two levels in my book *Energy Tapping*, I now believe that anything more than a simple trauma can be treated in the same way as highly complex trauma. Even simple traumas will respond to this more detailed tapping routine, which really only involves a few more tapping points and only a few more seconds of treatment. Before covering the details of this tapping technique, however, here's another example of its effectiveness:

■ Bill's Story: War Trauma

Bill was a Vietnam veteran who was decorated for his courage in battle. However, he bore the scars of war: an amputated left arm at the shoulder, breathing problems due to Agent Orange, alcohol and drug dependence, and many traumatic memories and nightmares. He had frequent flashbacks about fellow soldiers who died and enemy soldiers that he killed. He also felt hopeless and believed that he was guilty of mortal sins. Actually he was only defending himself in battle, but he still suffered guilt. Bill had been through therapy before, including therapy groups, emotional reliving, medication, chemical dependency treatment, and more. Regardless, he wasn't doing very well. His sister contacted me about seeing him.

Bill was exceptionally nervous at the initial session, expecting therapy to involve trips into the painful past, reliving scenes that he would prefer had never occurred in the first place. I explained that my kind of therapy is really different, and that I wouldn't require him to dwell on the past and become emotionally upset. I find that people benefit most from treatment if they are feeling more secure.

I explained the therapy process and that I would only ask him to briefly touch on painful memories, after which I would take him through a technique that could possibly take the distress away from the memory. As hard as it was for him to believe this, he went along with it anyway. Maybe he was just humoring me, or he was desperately seeking relief.

Bill mentioned one trauma that continued to haunt him since the war. He was engaged in hand-to-hand combat and killed the soldier with whom he was fighting. In the soldier's pocket, he found a photo of a woman and two children, which Bill assumed was the man's family. After Bill briefly told me about the event, he turned pale and began shaking. I then guided Bill to tap on several specific meridian points and to do the Brain Balancer. Within a few minutes, the memory of that event no longer bothered Bill. He could see what happened clearly, but color returned to his face and the shaking stopped. He was amazingly calm. Bewildered, he said, "It doesn't bother me! I can see what happened, but it doesn't bother me!" He no longer felt guilty about the event either. He could see clearly now that he had no choice other than to defend himself and his fellow soldiers at the time. I saw Bill many times over the next couple years and never again did that memory bother him.

I need to emphasize that resolving that traumatic memory was not sufficient to resolve all of Bill's problems. Treatment of many other traumatic memories and other issues was needed. However, he never experienced nightmares, flashbacks, or emotional distress about that specific memory again. And as treatment progressed, he experienced improvement in many other areas of his life as well.

Highly Complex Trauma Technique

The traumas of Barbara and Bill are examples of complex or highly complex trauma. Generally the following treatment works in situations where, like those of Barbara and Bill, there are many layers of trauma and distress. It is important to remember, as I mentioned earlier, that when a number of aspects are involved in the traumatic event, each aspect should be treated individually. Here is the technique to use for highly complex trauma:

1. Think about the event or specific aspect of the event and rate the discomfort level in any way you prefer (for example, SUD level 0 to 10, with 0 representing no discomfort and 10 representing the highest level of discomfort). This is a measure of how you presently feel as you think about the event, not the way you felt at the time that the event occurred.

2. Correct a possible reversal by tapping continually on the little-finger side of your hand (SH) or rubbing the sore spot (SS) on the left side of your chest while saying or thinking three times, "Even though I'm upset about what happened, I deeply and completely accept myself." You can be specific about the event. (See diagram 5: Energy Tapping for Highly Complex Trauma.)

3. Tap seven to ten times at each of the following meridian points: beginning of one or both eyebrows (EB) near the bridge of your nose, under one or both eyes (UE) on the bony orbit, six inches beneath one or both armpits (UA), under one or both collarbones next to your sternum (UCB), inside tip of either little fingernail (LF), under one or both collarbones next to your sternum (UCB), inside tip of either index fingernail (IF), under one or both collarbones next to your sternum (UCB). The sequence of points on the diagram is 1, 2, 3, 4, 5, 4, 6, and 4.

4. Reevaluate how you feel. If the discomfort level has decreased by at least 2 points, continue; otherwise repeat the psychological reversal treatment before continuing. In this case you will correct mini-reversal by tapping on the little-finger side of your hand (SH) while saying three times, "Even though I'm still upset about what happened, I deeply and completely accept myself."

5. To continue, do the Brain Balancer (BB) by tapping on the back of your hand (BH) between your little finger and ring finger while doing the following:

    Close your eyes.

    Open your eyes.

    Rotate your eyes in a circle clockwise while humming a tune.

    Rotate your eyes in a circle counterclockwise while multiplying any series of numbers, such as 12 × 2 = 24, 12 × 3 = 36, etc.

    Again, rotate your eyes in a circle clockwise while humming a tune.

6. Again evaluate how you feel. After doing the Brain Balancer (BB), your discomfort level will usually decrease, but there are instances where it will remain the same or increase. That's okay. If it increases, this sometimes means that you have tuned in another aspect of the problem. Just continue with the recipe.

7. Again tap seven to ten times at each of the following meridian points: beginning of one or both eyebrows (EB) near the bridge of your nose, under one or both eyes (UE) on the bony orbit, six inches beneath one or both armpits (UA), under one or both collarbones next to your sternum (UCB), inside tip of either little fingernail (LF), under one or both collarbones next to your sternum (UCB), inside tip of either index fingernail (IF), under one or both collarbones next to your sternum (UCB). The sequence of points on the diagram is 1, 2, 3, 4, 5, 4, 6, and 4.

8. Briefly check how you feel. The discomfort level should be even less at this point. If it is, continue to alternate among the eight treatment points (EB, UE, UA, UCB, LF, UCB, IF, UCB) and the Brain Balancer (BB) until the discomfort about the event is gone.

9. If progress comes to a standstill at any point, correct a possible mini-reversal by tapping on the little-finger side of your hand (SH) while saying three times, "Even though I'm still upset about what happened, I deeply and completely accept myself." Then continue alternating between the treatment points and the Brain Balancer (BB).

10. When your discomfort level is within the 0 to 2 range, it is often useful to add the Eye Roll (ER) or Elaborated Eye Roll (EER) one or a few times. For the ER, tap continually between your little finger and ring finger on the back of your hand (BH), slowly raise your eyes from the floor to the ceiling, take a slow deep breath, and then exhale. With the EER, also raise your

eyes upward while lowering your eyelids. Check to determine if there is any remaining discomfort.

11. If there isn't any discomfort, see if you can get it back. If you can, it means that there is an aspect that still needs to be treated. Continue with the technique.

Trauma Removal Technique (TRT)

Another helpful technique for dealing with highly complex trauma is the Trauma Removal Technique (TRT), which involves tapping at both the beginning and the

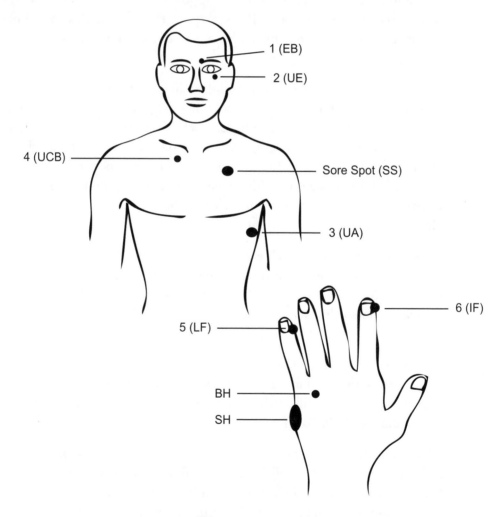

Diagram 5:
Energy Tapping for Highly Complex Trauma

Energy Tapping for Trauma

ending points of the meridians. Most EP techniques involve tapping on meridian points at locations such as the beginning of the eyebrow (EB), under collarbone (UCB), and so on. Usually you tap on one side or both sides of the body, such as both EB points. These treatment points are near the beginning or end of the meridians. For example, the bladder meridian has sixty seven points on both sides of the body that begin under the eyebrow (bladder-1) and extend to the outside of the little toenail (bladder-67). The beginning and ending points of the meridians are identified by the numbers so that number one on the bladder meridian is at the beginning and number sixty-seven is at the end. With the kidney meridian, number one is at the bottom of your foot and number twenty-seven is under your collarbone (UCB).

Generally, if you tap at the standard points, such as EB, UCB, and so on, you will get a decrease of stress connected to the issue being treated. But if this approach doesn't work well enough or at all, often a slightly more detailed approach will work. TRT involves tapping in sequence at or near the beginning and then at or near the ending points of the meridians. If you tap in this direction, you stimulate the meridians in the direction in which they are believed to naturally flow. In addition to the treatment points for reversal, the Brain Balancer (BB), and the Eye Roll (ER), I have generally found that the following paired points are sufficient to help you treat trauma and, in particular, highly complex trauma.

TRT TREATMENT POINTS

1. Eyebrow (EB): Beginning of each eyebrow at bridge of nose

2. Little Toenail (LT): Outside edge of the little toenails

3. Under Eye (UE): Bony orbits directly under each eye

4. Under Knee (UK): About four inches under front of each knee

5. Inner Ankle Bone (IA): Upper edge of the inner ankle bones

6. Under Collarbone (UCB): Next to sternum under the collarbones

7. Great Toenail (GT): Inside edge of big toenails

8. Under Arm (UA): Six inches under the armpits

9. Index Fingernail (IF): Thumb side of the index fingernails

10. Side of Nostril (SN): Either side of nose on the face

11. Armpit (A): Toward the front of each armpit

12. Little Fingernail (LF): Little fingernail facing the ring finger

Bring to mind an upsetting event and do the TRT now:

1. Think about the event, or a specific aspect of the event, and rate the discomfort level in any way you prefer (for example, SUD level 0 to 10, with 0 representing no discomfort and 10 representing the highest level of discomfort). This measures how you presently feel as you think about the event, not the way you felt at the time that the event occurred.

2. Treat for the possibility of reversal by tapping repeatedly on the side of your hand (SH) or rubbing the sore spot (SS) on the left side of your chest while thinking or saying three times, "Even though I am upset about _____, I deeply and completely accept myself." (Be specific about the event.) It may also prove helpful to tap the SH or rub the SS while saying, "I deeply and completely accept myself with all my problems and limitations." (See diagram 6: Trauma Removal Technique [TRT].)

3. While lightly thinking about the problem, tap seven to ten times at the sequence of each of these paired meridian points only hard enough to feel it: EB, LT → UE, UK → IA, UCB → GT, UA → IF, SN → A, LF. (See descriptions above and diagram 6 for treatment points.) On the diagram, the sequence of paired points is as follows:

    1, 2 → 3, 4 → 5, 6 → 7, 8 → 9, 10 → 11, 12

4. Again rate your level of discomfort. If there is no decrease, return to step 2 and cycle through the sequence again. It may be necessary to do this a few times before you start to experience some relief.

5. Next do the Brain Balancer (BB) by tapping continually at the back of your hand (BH) point while rotating your eyes clockwise, rotating your eyes counterclockwise, humming a tune, multiplying or dividing, and humming again.

6. Again rate your level of discomfort. If there is no decrease, return to step 2 and cycle through the sequence again. Sometimes it is necessary to do this a few times before you start to experience some relief.

7. Repeat the paired points: 1, 2 → 3, 4 → 5, 6 → 7, 8 → 9, 10 → 11, 12

8. Again rate your level of discomfort from 0 to 10. As long as the SUD level continues to decrease, do the TRT until there is little or no discomfort remaining. If the treatment stalls at any point, this may indicate a mini-reversal. Treat this reversal by tapping on the little-finger side of your hand

(SH) while saying three times, "Even though I still have some upset, I deeply and completely accept myself."

9. When your discomfort level is within the 0 to 2 range, it is often useful to add the Eye Roll (ER) or Elaborated Eye Roll (EER) one or a few times. For the ER, tap continually between your little finger and ring finger on the back of your hand (BH), slowly raise your eyes from the floor to the ceiling,

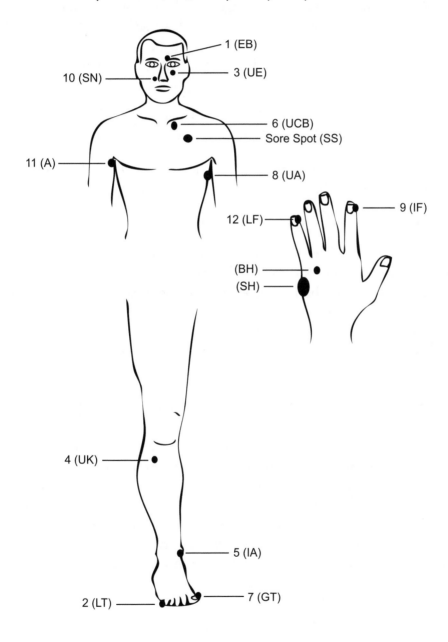

Diagram 6: Trauma Removal Technique (TRT)

take a slow deep breath, and then exhale. With the EER, raise your eyes upward while lowering your eyelids.

10. Again rate your level of discomfort. When the SUD is 0 to 1, challenge the results: see if you can get back to any distress. If you can, the treatment is not entirely complete and you should repeat the sequence.

11. When you are within the 0 to 1 range, consider what would you like to experience and believe now that the discomfort has been removed. For example, before the treatment, you may have felt that you couldn't go on with your life, but now you would like to believe that you are resilient and can embrace life fully.

12. Rate how convinced you are of this, with 0 indicating that you do not believe this at all and 10 indicating that you absolutely believe this.

13. Tap on the back of your hand (BH) while instilling this belief. Instillation can be done by verbalizing or visualizing the belief.

14. Intermittently rate your level of conviction until the range is 8 to 10.

15. When the level of conviction is within the 8 to 10 range, do the Elaborated Eye Roll (EER) to complete the treatment effects. To do this, tap on the back of your hand (BH) while holding your head straight and slowly move your eyes from the floor to the ceiling. Once your eyes are pointed at the ceiling, maintain your gaze upward while lowering your eyelids and taking a deep breath. At this point, stop tapping, exhale, and relax.

Global Techniques for Trauma and Other Disorders

The three ET recipes covered above are specifically designed to treat trauma. However, there are other EP techniques that can be used to resolve trauma as well as other disorders such as phobias, depression, panic, feelings of worthlessness, and addictive urges. We call them "global" techniques because of the wide range of problems they can treat. We'll look at one of those global techniques—Midline Energy Treatment—after an example of how I used it to help a trauma survivor. Amanda is just one of many people whom I have treated successfully with this technique.

Amanda's Story: Car Accident and Molestation Trauma

Amanda, a nineteen-year-old female university student, was referred to me because of PTSD after an automobile accident. The driver in the other car crossed over the median strip and struck her vehicle head-on, killing both of his passengers and himself. Amanda was pinned under the dashboard for several hours while a rescue team used the Jaws of Life to get her out of her crushed car. She suffered multiple injuries, and was in the hospital and then a rehabilitation center for several months. I saw her a year after the accident. At that time, she was having frequent nightmares, flashbacks, panic, anxiety, and guilt feelings. She was also abusing alcohol.

Initially we focused on her memory of being pinned under the dashboard. After she thought about it and rated the discomfort as a 9 on a 0 to 10 scale, I asked her to dismiss the memory from her mind while following the Midline Energy Treatment (MET), a global technique I developed many years ago. MET involves physically tapping on four points on the head and chest (related to acupoints and chakras): third eye (TE), under nose (UN), under bottom lip (UBL), and on the upper chest (CH). After about five rounds of tapping, she was able to vividly recall the event without discomfort. Several times throughout treatment, she laughed and asked me, "How does that work?" Follow-up sessions at one week, two weeks, and two months revealed that after the initial session, distress about the event, nightmares, and flashbacks no longer occurred.

During the course of treatment, other aspects of the trauma were treated, including feelings of guilt about the people who died. That distress was also resolved in one session by using MET and a couple of related treatments.

Later in therapy, she reported that a relative molested her from age five to twelve. Using a more specifically focused treatment that includes manual muscle testing, we were able to determine which meridians were involved in order to efficiently eliminate this abuse trauma. After we treated upset connected to various memories, she reported a lingering feeling of worthlessness, including a "dirty and disgusting" feeling in the lower abdomen. We were able to eliminate this sensation as well as her belief about not being worthwhile. A follow-up, several months and a couple of years later, revealed that Amanda was experiencing ongoing relief.

Midline Energy Treatment (MET)

In the early 1990s, I developed the Negative Affect Erasing Method (NAEM)™, which is more descriptively called the Midline Energy Treatment (MET). My clients and many therapists have found it to be highly effective in the treatment of different kinds of psychological problems, such as trauma, phobias, anxiety, depression, and a number of other conditions. I have also found it effective for eliminating negative core beliefs and instilling positive ones.

Like other techniques covered in this book, you will find MET quite simple to learn. It entails many of the same features that are common to other EP techniques. That is, when needed, you can correct reversal or switching and use the Brain Balancer (BB) and Eye Roll (ER) techniques.

The four MET treatment points are the following:

TE = Third-eye point, between and slightly above the eyebrows

UN = Under nose

UBL = Under bottom lip

CH = Upper part of the sternum on the chest (over the thymus gland)

The inspiration for developing MET was rather simple. I found that these points were highly robust, often regardless of the condition being treated. The third-eye point has been discussed for ages and is thought to be related to the pineal gland, which is located between the hemispheres at the center of the brain. French philosopher René Descartes thought that the pineal gland was the "seat of the soul." Now we know that it is important in the production of melatonin, which is a powerful antioxidant and important in the sleep-wake cycle. The third-eye point is also the location of the sixth chakra, which is assumed to be relevant to insight. At this location, many Asian men and women wear a forehead decoration called a "bindi," which is said to cool and soothe the soul. The points under the nose and bottom lip are ending points for the governing and central vessels, respectively. The governing vessel is an energy pathway that travels the length of your back, over your head, and ends under your upper lip. The central vessel is on the front of your body, with the last point being at the bottom lip. These vessels interact with the entire meridian system and are often stimulated in applied kinesiology (AK) to treat a condition referred to as switching. Switching is a pervasive energy disorganization that can prevent treatment from working. It is covered in detail in chapters 4 and 6.

Finally, the chest (CH) point is on the thymus gland, which is important in the immune system. Psychiatrist John Diamond (1985) considered the thymus to be the regulator gland of the meridian system.

The MET Technique

1. Think about the event, or a specific aspect of the event, and rate the discomfort level in any way you prefer (for example, SUD level 0 to 10, with 0 representing no discomfort and 10 representing the highest level of discomfort). This is a measure of how you presently feel as you think about the event, not the way you felt at the time that the event occurred.

2. Treat for the possibility of reversal by tapping repeatedly on the side of your hand (SH) or rubbing the sore spot (SS) on the left side of your chest while thinking or saying three times, "Even though I am upset, I deeply and completely accept myself." (Be specific.) It may also prove helpful to tap the SH or rub the SS while saying, "I deeply and completely accept myself with all my problems and limitations." (See diagram 7: Midline Energy Treatment [MET].)

3. While lightly thinking about the problem, tap seven to ten times at each of these meridian points: TE, UN, UBL, and CH (numbers 1, 2, 3, and 4 on the diagram). Tap only hard enough to feel it.

4. Again rate your level of discomfort. If there is no decrease, return to step 2 and cycle through the sequence again. Sometimes it is necessary to do this a few times before you start to experience some relief.

5. Next do the Brain Balancer (BB) by tapping continually at the back of your hand (BH) point while rotating your eyes clockwise, rotating your eyes counterclockwise, humming a tune, multiplying or dividing, and humming again.

6. Repeat the tapping sequence: TE, UN, UBL, and CH.

7. Again rate your level of discomfort from 0 to 10. It should be lower yet. When the discomfort is within the 0 to 2 range, go to step 9. Sometimes it will be necessary to repeat the treatment several times while you think about the event or while you are in situations that trigger memories of the event before you feel complete relief.

8. As long as the discomfort level continues to decrease, proceed with the MET technique until there is little or no discomfort remaining. If the treatment stalls at any point, this may indicate a mini-reversal. Treat this reversal by tapping on the little-finger side of your hand (SH) while saying three times, "Even though I still have some upset, I deeply and completely accept myself."

9. When your discomfort level is within the 0 to 2 range, it is often useful to add the Eye Roll (ER) or Elaborated Eye Roll (EER) one or a few times. For the ER, tap continually between your little finger and ring finger on the back of your hand (BH), slowly raise your eyes from the floor to the ceiling, take a slow deep breath, and then exhale. With the EER, also raise your eyes upward while lowering your eyelids.

10. Again rate your level of discomfort. If it is a 0, you are done for now. However, consider challenging the results by seeing if you can get back to any distress. If you can, the treatment is not entirely complete and you should repeat the sequence.

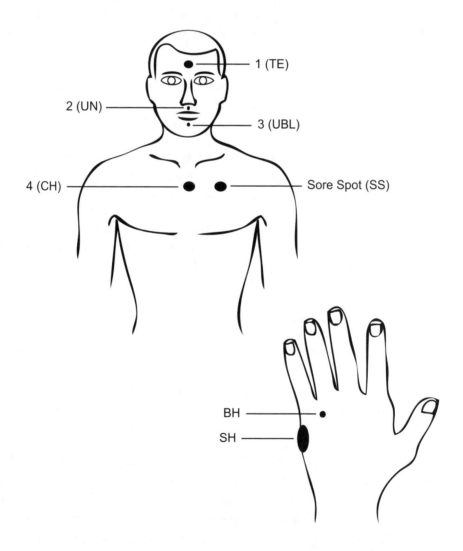

Diagram 7: Midline Energy Treatment (MET)

Energy Tapping for Trauma

Eight-Step Process (ESP)

In the early 2000s, I developed the Eight-Step Process (ESP). Many people have found it to be highly effective in the treatment of a variety of problems, such as trauma, phobias, anxiety, depression, peak-performance issues, and more. I have also found it effective for general stress reduction and changing limiting core beliefs. Like other techniques covered in this book, you will find ESP quite simple to learn.

The eight ESP treatment positions are the following:

1. Butterfly Hug

2. Chest Gliding

3. Chest Holding

4. Chest/Forehead Holding

5. Frontal/Occipital Holding (FOH)

6. Chest/Occipital Holding

7. Chest Holding

8. Acceptance Gesture

ESP integrates many separate techniques that have been commonly used by various people and employed in several therapeutic fields for decades. I find this process to be highly robust and applicable to many types of psychological issues. The butterfly hug involves bilateral stimulation and helps to coordinate left and right hemispheres of your brain. This technique has also been used by therapists who do eye movement desensitization and reprocessing (EMDR). Chest gliding settles stress symptoms because of the downward movement at your midline, which is where most people report feeling emotions. Chest holding is a universal gesture that also has a soothing effect, especially if you focus your attention on your heart and away from any distressing thoughts while doing this. Chest/forehead holding combines the effects of chest holding with elements of emotional stress release (ESR), both powerful stress-reducing techniques. This step shifts your focus and may also promote balance between the heart and the frontal areas of the brain, which is the location of decision making and other executive functions. Frontal/occipital holding (FOH) is the next step in the series, which was also discussed earlier in this chapter as a stress-reduction technique used in many branches of kinesiology. Just as the butterfly hug coordinates the left and right cerebral hemispheres, FOH may additionally serve to create balance between the front and back of the brain. Chest/occipital holding involves holding the back of your head and the center of your chest. This position serves to further reduce stress by shifting focus and may promote balance between the heart and the occipital region of the brain. Next, you resume the chest holding position. The final step is a universal gesture of acceptance and love that is described as a "high-thymus gesture" (Diamond 1985). This gesture promotes openness, since it begins with a closed gesture (arms crossed over the chest) and then there is an opening, with your arms extended outward.

I used ESP with my client Carl, who had suffered a serious head injury. His experience illustrates the effectiveness of the Eight-Step Process.

■ Carl's Story: Head-Injury Trauma

Carl was fifty-two years old and one of the most extreme type A personalities I'd ever met. He even referred to himself as quadruple type A. He was a powerhouse salesperson. Twelve times in a row he made salesperson of the month. And as we usually think of type As, he talked fast and could be impatient. But still he was an all-round nice guy and a brilliant networker. Then the tragic event happened. One February morning, he slipped on ice in the parking lot at work and fell, suffering a severe concussion. He was taken to the hospital by ambulance and remained there overnight for tests and observation. After this incident, he was off work for several months and was under the care of a neurologist. As a result of his head injury, he had problems with attention, concentration, short-term memory, and coordination. Frequently he stumbled and dropped things. He had difficulty recalling the correct word when talking, forgot names and appointments, and generally had "working memory" (the current term for short-term memory) deficits. Prior to this closed-head injury, which is also called mild traumatic brain injury (MTBI), Carl had none of these problems. His memory had been impeccable, and most people were amazed at his agile recall of names, faces, numbers, and other details. He also enjoyed golfing and a game of basketball with his sons and neighborhood kids.

Most people associate PTSD with war, rape, mugging, natural disasters, terrorist acts, and similar experiences. But even a personal injury like Carl's can result in emotional as well as physical trauma. He was distressed about his injury and had flashbacks and recurrent nightmares. He was referred to me by his neurologist with the request that I provide evaluation and treatment. I began by interviewing Carl and administering a battery of neuropsychological tests. These tests are useful in evaluating memory, concentration, eye-hand coordination, and other neuropsychological elements, and for gauging recovery progress after a trauma. The testing was consistent with extensive cognitive deficits and PTSD symptoms.

Carl was experiencing distress about the incident of slipping on ice and the events that followed. Within the course of a few sessions, we were able to easily resolve his distress about a number of the traumatic scenes by using a couple ET techniques, including the Trauma Removal Technique (TRT). Shortly after beginning therapy, he returned to work even though he had persistent cognitive and coordination problems. It was his idea to return to work, since he felt that he wouldn't get better "just sitting around the house and going for walks." However, he felt stressed that he would not be able to perform at the level he did prior to his injury and worried that he would be placed on disability.

At this point, I asked Carl to tune in to the distress he was feeling and I took him through the Eight-Step Process (ESP). With each round of this technique, he processed and resolved layer after layer of emotional issues. The issues included fear that he wouldn't be able to perform well on the job, then fear that he would lose his job, then embarrassment about being on disability, and then anger, and then sadness and despair that he "wouldn't amount to anything." Interestingly, at this point Carl recalled several events with his father when he was a teenager. It seems that his father was also type A and he could be quite harsh and demeaning toward Carl. "You won't amount to anything," he would say when he was frustrated with Carl's behavior and less-than-stellar school performance. Carl was stunned to recall this during the process. He realized that his own type A and workaholic behaviors were connected with wanting to prove his father wrong and to earn his father's approval. Also he realized that his fears about not performing up to snuff at work were rooted in distorted self-esteem issues.

Carl resolved his fears and also the embedded trauma that he had been living with for so many years. By the close of therapy, his performance at work was improving, to a large extent because he was not living in perpetual fear about his performance. He also shifted out of quadruple type A, and instead he learned to smell the roses and appreciate the virtues of patience. When I last saw him, he still had some cognitive deficits, but he found many effective ways to compensate for this. He also came to view his head trauma as "a wake-up call that knocked some sense" into him. He had an amazing shift in how he saw his trauma. He truly believed that it helped him to know what life is really all about.

Here's the technique I used with Carl and many other people. You can use it for stress reduction and to treat specific issues such as trauma. This process integrates bilateral stimulation to coordinate the hemispheres of your brain (butterfly hug), rubbing and holding at the midline to settle distress and promote calmness (chest gliding and chest holding), variations of emotional stress release (ESR), and a gesture that signals acceptance and letting go. So bring to mind another memory that still causes some level of discomfort and do the ESP.

Eight-Step Process Technique

Before you begin the eight steps, you'll do some familiar preparation techniques:

Think about the event, or a specific aspect of the event, and rate the discomfort level in any way you prefer (for example, SUD level 0 to 10, with 0 representing no discomfort and 10 representing the highest level of discomfort). This measures how you presently feel as you think about the event, not the way you felt at the time that the event occurred.

Treat for the possibility of reversal by tapping repeatedly on the side of your hand (SH) or rubbing the sore spot (SS) on the left side of your chest while thinking or saying three times, "Even though I am upset about _____, I deeply and completely accept myself." (Be specific about the event.) It may also prove helpful to tap the SH or rub the SS while saying, "I deeply and completely accept myself with all my problems and limitations."

1. While lightly thinking about the problem, do the butterfly hug for about twenty seconds. To do this, cross your arms over your chest with each hand touching a shoulder and then alternately tap each shoulder. Pay attention to your emotional issue and the feeling of your hands alternately tapping each shoulder.

2. For about twenty seconds, do chest gliding by sliding your hands one after another over the center of your chest, as if you were smoothing out your shirt or blouse. Pay attention to your emotional issue and the feeling of your hands alternately gliding over your chest.

3. Next, do chest holding for about twenty seconds by placing one hand atop the other at the center of your chest. Pay attention to your emotional issue and the feeling of your hands over your chest.

4. Then do chest/forehead holding by keeping the bottom hand on your chest and moving the top hand to your forehead, holding this position for about twenty seconds. Pay attention to your emotional issue and the feeling of your hands touching your chest and forehead.

5. Then do frontal/occipital holding (FOH) by keeping your hand on your forehead and placing your other hand at the back of your head, holding this pose for about twenty seconds. Pay attention to your emotional issue and the feeling of your hands holding the front and back of your head.

6. Next, take your hand off your forehead and return it to your chest, keeping your other hand at the back of your head. Maintain this chest/occipital

holding position for about twenty seconds. Pay attention to your emotional issue and the feeling of your hands touching your chest and the back of your head.

7. Now take your hand off the back of your head and place it on the hand on your chest (chest holding), maintaining this pose for about twenty seconds. Pay attention to your emotional issue and the feeling of your hands over your chest.

8. Finally, return to the butterfly hug, but this time simply hold the position for a few seconds and then slowly extend your arms and hands outward in an acceptance gesture while saying "Trauma be gone." Repeat this gesture and phrase two more times.

Reevaluate how you feel about the event and repeat the process each time another aspect or new issue emerges.

You can also use the ESP as a general stress reducer and energy balancer. Rather than bringing to mind a traumatic memory or other emotionally distressing issue, just notice how you feel in the moment and rate your level of stress 0 to 10. Then do ESP and reevaluate your stress level. You can add extra benefits to the technique if you combine Alpha-Theta Breathing with ESP. Enjoy!

Despite the frequent effectiveness of the techniques covered in this chapter, at times they do not work as well as you would like. A number of things can interfere with the effectiveness of the techniques. Troubleshooting will help you discover where the problems are and how to deal with them. So now we turn to chapter 6 to learn how to troubleshoot and fine-tune ET.

6

Troubleshooting

If you do what you've always done, you'll get what you've always gotten.

—Anthony Robbins

Most of the time ET techniques will work amazingly well in helping you remove negative emotions and other symptoms of trauma. You simply tune in, do a SUD rating or just notice your discomfort level, and then stimulate your body in one or more of the ways covered in chapter 5. This is truly a mind-body approach, and I believe that's the way therapy works at its best. The mind and body are not separate, so any therapeutic approach that does not take this unity into account is incomplete. The same applies to medicine in general. It's essential to treat the whole person if deep healing is to occur. More about this in the last two chapters.

Despite the general effectiveness of ET techniques, there are times when you may not get the results you want, even though you follow the techniques to the letter. When that happens, you'll need to troubleshoot, which you'll learn how to do in this chapter. The following ideas and techniques will help you to get the most out of EP and ET. Familiarize yourself with the suggestions first so that you'll have a better idea of what to do when a particular technique is not working as exquisitely as you would like it to. Although each of these suggestions is listed under a particular category, they often overlap. In other words, a particular recommendation could easily be listed in more than one category.

Thoroughness

It is important for you to be persistent and to test the thoroughness of your results after using ET techniques. One round of ET is seldom sufficient. Many traumas contain numerous aspects or scenes, and it's important for you to remove the traumatic stress from all of them in order to feel your best.

Repetition: Keep on Tapping

Usually persistence pays off. As Thomas H. Palmer wrote in 1840 in *The Teacher's Manual*, "If at first you don't succeed, try, try again." So keep in mind that sometimes you need to use an ET technique many times on the same trauma or other problem before you get relief and lasting results. Sometimes the trauma involves several layers, and each needs to be treated before experiencing total relief.

Results Testing (Challenging)

After using an ET technique, you may feel much more relaxed and find that the traumatic memory no longer bothers you. However, later you may find that thoughts about the event or certain situations that remind you of it will trigger some level of distress. This means you have not yet thoroughly treated the trauma. To prevent recurrence at a later time, it's a good idea to challenge the results whenever you get the SUD down to 0. Simply try to make the trauma bother you again. You can search for different scenes or aspects of scenes that you haven't yet thoroughly treated. If you feel some level of discomfort, hold that aspect in mind and do the treatment again. Your goal is to get to the point where no matter how much you try, you cannot feel any discomfort about the event.

Flexibility

Even after considerable repetition, your results of using ET techniques may not be sufficient. If you try, try again and still don't succeed, try something else. As my good friend Anthony Robbins says, "If you do what you've always done, you'll get what you've always gotten." So it makes sense that if you try a technique several times and it doesn't give you the results you're looking for, move on to another strategy. The more choices you have, the more likely you will get the results you want. So read on!

Preparation

Before treating a trauma, it makes sense to be in an optimal state. If you are hungry, thirsty, tired, overly stressed, or in a "bad place" in any other way, you may find it difficult or impossible to get the ET techniques to work. Here are a few simple ways to significantly improve your chances of getting the results you want:

Drink Water

Sometimes the ET techniques work better after you drink a glass of water. There could be many reasons for this. If you are thirsty or experiencing some level of dehydration, that appears to interfere with the effectiveness of the techniques. This may be due to the fact that water is an electrical conductor and drinking water helps to facilitate the conduction of signals through your body, including the signal created through tapping. Also, swallowing water is often soothing, and this in and of itself helps to reduce stress. The downward "motility" (contractions) of your esophagus is called "peristalsis," and peristalsis can also reduce anxiety. If you eat when you are stressed, this is partly why you eat at such times—because the peristalsis helps reduce stress. Instead of eating when you feel stressed, consider tapping and drinking water instead. This gives a whole new meaning to the term "tap water."

First Things First

If you try to treat a trauma and you experience something that interferes with your focus—another emotion, a different memory, a physical need—it's important to take care of that first. For example, if you are tired, hungry, or stressed, you will find it very difficult to effectively treat the trauma. Take care of the present issue first, before attempting to treat the trauma. If you are stressed, consider using frontal/occipital holding (FOH) or the Midline Energy Treatment (MET) to help you relax. These techniques reduce stress and allow you to focus on the trauma that you wish to resolve.

Deep Breathing

Sometimes it's helpful to do some deep breathing during the course of tapping. Deep breathing reduces sympathetic nervous system activation and produces more alpha and theta waves. For more details, see chapter 5.

Switching (Neurologic Disorganization)

Generally when treating a problem with ET, the SUD decreases fairly quickly and in significant increments of a few points after each treatment. However, if you are treating a trauma and your SUD lowers very slowly, perhaps only one point or a fraction of a point with each round of tapping or other ET technique, you may be experiencing what people working in the field of applied kinesiology (AK) refer to as switching or neurologic disorganization. This condition involves pervasive energy disorganization. When you are switched, your energy system is disrupted and therefore you are unable to benefit from the treatments effectively, and sometimes not at all. Switching appears to involve the central nervous system (CNS) misinterpreting and misconstruing nerve impulses. Obviously a disturbance in the signaling system between your CNS and the rest of your body would greatly impair your ability to focus and navigate. An obvious example of this is people who have attention-deficit/hyperactivity disorder (ADHD), which makes it very difficult for them to learn because of their inability to focus. When you experience switching, you might find it difficult to follow directions, or you may frequently bump into things or say the wrong word when talking. There can be other reasons for these symptoms, but switching is one of them.

Several techniques correct switching for brief and often extended periods of time. Two ways that can help you correct switching are the Hook-Up Technique, which was described in chapter 4 (repeated here for your convenience) and the Collarbone-Navel Technique. Give them a try.

HOOK-UP TECHNIQUE

1. Sit in a chair, extend your legs in front of you on the floor, and cross your left ankle over your right.

2.   Extend your arms in front of you with the backs of your hands touching. Next, raise your right hand up and over your left so that the palms are touching and interlock your fingers. Lower your arms and then raise them so that your hands now rest on your chest.

3.   While holding this position, place your tongue to the roof of your mouth about one-half inch behind your upper teeth.

4.   Slowly breathe in through your nose and out through your mouth for approximately one minute.

5.   After doing the Hook-Up Technique, resume tapping. The SUD will then often decrease more efficiently.

COLLARBONE-NAVEL TECHNIQUE

1.   Place one of your hands over your navel. With the thumb and fingers of your other hand, briskly massage under your collarbones close to the chest bone (sternum) and breathe deeply for about twenty seconds.

2.   Switch hands and repeat for about twenty seconds.

3.   After doing this technique, resume tapping. The SUD will then often decrease more efficiently.

Psychological Reversal

In chapter 4, you learned about psychological reversal. Since reversal is such an important issue, some of that information is repeated here. In short, psychological reversal means that your whole self is not aligned with or committed to your goal. When you are reversed, you want to resolve your trauma or other problem, but a part of you resists that. Often another issue lies in front of or is intertwined with the issue that you are trying to treat. Because of that interference, reversal seems to misalign your energy. You then do the opposite of what you consciously say you want to do.

Often reversal can be corrected by doing the exercise below:

KARATE-CHOPPING EXERCISE

Continually tap the little-finger side of one of your hands against the palm of your other hand (karate-chopping style), or tap your fists together with clenched fingers facing you while saying several times in a convincing tone:

"Even though I have this trauma, I deeply and completely accept myself."

(Even though this should be said in a convincing tone, be aware that you don't necessarily have to believe it for it to be effective.) Alternatively, you can use a phrase such as:

"Even though I have this trauma, I deeply and completely accept myself, and I'm willing to resolve this trauma."

Sometimes the reversal shows up as an issue concerning your ability to get over the trauma or the appropriateness of getting over the trauma. For example, a part of you might feel that you don't deserve to get over it, or that it's not safe to get over it, or that it's impossible to get over it, or that you would be violating a sense of loyalty to someone if you got over it, and so on. These issues can be treated by using the same basic technique but changing the wording as follows:

"Even if I don't deserve to get over this trauma, I deeply and completely accept myself."

"Even if a part of me believes it's impossible for me to get over this trauma, I deeply and completely accept myself, and I'm willing to get over this trauma."

"Even if it isn't safe for me to get over this trauma, I deeply and completely accept myself, and I choose to get over this trauma."

"Even if a part of me believes that I would not be loyal to (person's name) by getting over this trauma, I deeply and completely accept myself, and I'm willing to get over this trauma."

As also noted in chapter 4, sometimes the Karate-Chopping Exercise does not work to correct the reversal. In these cases, other places to tap that may work include the following (see diagram 2: Psychological Reversal Correction Points):

- The sore spot (SS), which is a tender spot on the left side of your chest, between the second and third ribs above the breast.

- Under your nose (UN)

- Under your bottom lip (UBL)

- Under your collarbones next to the sternum (UCB)

- Upper portion of the center of your chest (CH)

- Back of your hand between the little and ring fingers (BH)

- Under your eyes (UE) on the bony orbit of the cheekbone

It is not always necessary to use an affirmation to treat reversal. If the SUD is not decreasing while you are treating a trauma, assume that you have a reversal. Tap one or several of the correction points listed above and hold the intention of removing the reversal. Then resume the ET treatment for the trauma.

Frequently you can sense your own ambivalence about getting over the trauma. Look for the thought at the root of the feeling. You might feel that it's impossible to get over the trauma or perhaps that you'd be letting somebody off the hook if you got over it. Or you might feel angry at yourself. When you sense these interfering thoughts and feelings, treat them first with one of the techniques we covered in chapter 5, such as the Midline Energy Treatment (MET) or the Eight-Step Process (ESP). Also, you can rate the SUD of this issue from 0 to 10, with 10 being the strongest level of intensity, and then tap one or several of the reversal correction points until you notice that the interference has been eliminated. Remember that as long as you are reversed, treatment cannot go forward.

Attunement

Attunement or tuning in is simply thinking about or bringing to mind the trauma or specific scene or aspect that you want to treat. If you use an ET technique without aiming in the right direction—that is, without adequately tuning in—you'll probably feel more relaxed, but you'll miss your target. Precise attunement is important for resolving your trauma. Let's look at a couple of ways—scene and aspect naming, and leg locking—that will help you be certain that you are adequately attuned.

Scene and Aspect Naming

Sometimes when doing an ET technique, you can lose track of what you're treating. Obviously this can interfere with getting the results you want, so it's important to maintain focus on the trauma while treating it. This doesn't mean that you should get caught up in reliving the trauma, but the trauma does need to be tuned in at some level. One way to do this is to identify the scene or aspect that you're treating and give it a name or use a phrase to describe it. Then, while doing an ET technique, occasionally say or think the name or descriptive phrase. My good friend Gary Craig calls these "reminder phrases." For example, you might at times use the general terms "this trauma" or "that problem." To attune more precisely, try being more specific. For example, depending on your particular trauma, you might use words and phrases such as "my sadness," "my accident," "terrified," "the tornado," "the tornado ripping apart my house," or "my guilt." In short, think about the scene or aspect, and then give it a name or phrase to help you stay focused while treating the trauma.

Leg Locking

Another way to keep the problem in focus without reliving it is to use leg locking. This technique anchors or locks in the energetic information about the trauma in your body. It's quite simple, so give it a try now.

LEG-LOCK TECHNIQUE

1. Bring the trauma, scene, or other aspect to mind.

2. Rate the SUD level 0 to 10.

3. Stand with your feet close together.

4. Turn your feet outward with the heels together to make a V.

5. Extend one leg outward so that your feet are now about two feet apart.

6. Again momentarily think about the event and then bring your feet back to the V position in step 4.

7. While holding this position (either standing or sitting), do your preferred ET technique.

Treatment Strategies for Success

Several treatment strategies or "protocols" can increase your chances of success in resolving single-incident and multiple traumas. These strategies will help you treat your trauma thoroughly—we talked about the importance of thoroughness earlier in this chapter—and also help you to resolve it in the least upsetting ways.

Most Significant Scene

Sometimes it is enough to address the most significant scene or scenes of the traumatic memory. This can usually be determined by rating the SUD level, since the most significant scene will usually be the most emotionally intense. Treating that particular scene will significantly reduce and sometimes even eliminate the distress of the entire trauma. The significant scene is the linchpin, so to speak, that holds the trauma together.

Follow the Scenes

In most cases, a trauma does not occur in a single moment. It involves both many moments in time and many scenes. For example, I treated a man a number of years ago who had suffered an awful event. He and his wife were drinking at a party and they had an argument. After returning to their home, they had a brutal argument that led to her shooting herself. He was in another room when he heard the shot coming from the kitchen and quickly returned to the kitchen to see her lying on the floor. He called his brother, who then told him to call 911. After he called 911, the police arrived with the ambulance and, thinking that he'd shot his wife, arrested him, placing him in handcuffs. Shortly after they saw that he did not shoot his wife, they removed the cuffs. Throughout this series of events, he also saw his wife lying on the kitchen floor in a puddle of blood. Many other upsetting events followed. To help him resolve the trauma, I had him follow the scenes one by one, each time rating the SUD and then doing ET for highly complex trauma until he could look at each scene without distress. We proceeded one scene after another, erasing the distress. In many instances, this is what you can do to effectively treat a trauma with many scenes and aspects. Follow the sequence of events and treat them one at a time until you can look at the entire event without any distress.

Least to Most Intense Scene

In some cases, you will be able to resolve a trauma much easier if you determine the level of discomfort associated with each scene and then start with the least intense, working your way up to the most intense. For example, if there are five scenes involved in a trauma, the SUD levels might be 4, 5, 6, 8, and 10. When using this strategy, begin with the scene that is at level 4 and do not move on to the next most intense scene until this one has been resolved. This approach is similar to systematic desensitization, developed by Dr. Joseph Wolpe (see chapter 2). You form a hierarchy from the least uncomfortable to the most uncomfortable, which allows you to resolve and heal the less painful aspects of your trauma first. This foundation of healing allows you to address progressively more distressing aspects of the trauma, experiencing resolution and healing at each step along the way. Using this strategy with the suicide trauma discussed above, the least intense scene might have been the argument that the man had with his wife at the party and the most intense scene would be when he saw her body lying on the kitchen floor.

Specific Emotions and Thoughts

As we've said before, usually a trauma is made up of many scenes, emotions, and thoughts. In most cases, you will find that your thoughts are associated with specific emotions, such as anger, guilt, shame, or fear. The thoughts that you have about the trauma are a kind of commentary about it. For example, someone might think "How stupid I am" or "God will never forgive me." So there can be a specific scene in addition to something that you think about the scene. While treating the scene will often change the thought and the emotion, at other times you need to specifically target the thought and the emotion together in order to eliminate distress about the event.

Earliest Trauma

Sometimes what makes a traumatic event and the memory all the more intense is its similarity to another event that happened earlier in your life. This relationship is sometimes obvious if you find yourself saying something like "Why does this always happen to me?" or "This is just like that." It is important to be aware of this relationship and how the distress of the earlier trauma "feeds" into the later trauma. Often you can successfully treat a recent trauma without having to treat the earlier trauma. However, when the recent trauma is not resolving efficiently, this may be a sign that a "feeder" trauma needs to be dealt with first.

Dissociation and Introjects

It's common to dissociate during a severe traumatic event, which provides a level of protection or insulation from intense fear. Basically, *dissociation* involves mentally "leaving" your body, but the effects can linger and later cause you to dissociate in everyday life; this can, among other things, cause relationship problems. (We'll go into ways of countering dissociation below, but it's important for you to know that treating trauma with energy tapping goes a long way toward helping you to remain present.)

When you dissociate during a trauma, you can also "introject," which means incorporating characteristics of a person, animal, or object into your mental functioning. If, for example, a trauma is the result of another person harming you, you may introject characteristics of that person so that in some ways you unconsciously "become" that person. I realize that this sounds very strange and maybe even esoteric, but it does happen. When this is the case, simply treating the trauma from your own point of view may not be enough. Sometimes it is necessary to do the technique while imagining yourself being the person, animal, or thing that traumatized you.

I learned about this several years ago while training a number of therapists from Yugoslavia to help people traumatized by war. One therapist who was using ET reported that he had not been successful in treating a woman who had been raped until he had her imagine that she was the soldier who raped her. Admittedly, it took a lot of explanation, encouragement, and support to help her do this, but using the treatment while she maintained the perceptual position of the rapist is what eliminated the trauma. Probably in most cases like this, the assistance of a therapist is needed.

Helpful Variations for Body Stimulation

In addition to simply tapping on treatment points, a number of variations may be useful when you are not getting adequate results. This includes changing the tapping pattern and stimulating your body in other ways. Because each of us is different, it's important to experiment to discover what variations work best for you.

Tapping Frequency and Intensity

The speed and intensity with which you tap may affect the results you get. For example, you may get better results when you tap slower rather than faster, and vice versa. When you are tapping at a certain rate, consider changing the tapping pattern to see if this makes a difference in lowering your SUD rating. Try tapping fast, moderately, or slowly. Sometimes slower tapping is more calming, but this can be a matter of personal preference. Compare the effects of tapping harder, softer, or very lightly. You may also find different rhythmic patterns more effective, such as tapping in a waltz beat or the beat of a favorite song.

Alternatives to Tapping

In my experience, tapping is generally the most powerful way of changing the SUD rating. If you find tapping irritating, however, consider one of the other methods of stimulating the treatment points. For example, you can rub in a circular motion at the treatment points, or simply touch the points with a certain amount of pressure. Other methods include holding the points while taking some deep breaths or flicking the points. After you have physically stimulated the treatment points, you'll find that it is often effective to simply imagine tapping the points or simply mentally focusing on those locations whenever it's not convenient to tap. I discovered this many years ago after a number of clients reported to me that they no longer needed to tap, that they only had to think about it in order for it to work. When I inquired further, I discovered that they were imagining tapping and would actually get a feeling as though they were tapping. Try it!

Body Movements

Sometimes you can make the ET techniques more powerful by adding other body movements. For example, while tapping, you might walk or run, stretch, hop, or do some other movement. When you tap, you send electrical signals to your brain and other body locations. This disrupts your thoughts of the trauma that you are tuning in and helps to change its structure. Adding other body movements can further intensify this effect. Of course, the range of movements will be restricted if you are also using the Leg-Lock Technique.

Preventing Upset

You may experience distress if you focus too intensely on your traumatic memory while using ET. This is like having surgery without an anesthesia, which is not such a good idea. Here are a few things you can do to remain more comfortable when treating a trauma:

Being Present

Intense emotional reactions are understandable and common when recalling a traumatic event. While reliving a trauma in therapy can be curative at times, this is, as I said above, like undergoing surgery without anesthesia. Also, if you burned your hand on a stove, your doctor wouldn't tell you that putting your hand back on the hot stove would help it. A more sensible prescription would be to apply a burn ointment and bandage, and protect your hand from injury. When emotional reliving works, it seems like the intense emotion was necessary for resolving the trauma. But the curative factor is being able to focus on what happened rather than avoiding it, and then being able to think and feel differently about it.

There are many ways to help prevent severe emotional reactions when treating a trauma. One method you can use before tuning in and treating the trauma is to engage in a number of physical movements. Try this exercise now if you can.

WHOLE-BODY EXERCISE

Begin by stretching your body. Raise your arms above your head and stretch. Lean over and stretch. Stretch from side to side. Then twist your body in different directions. Do the "twist," Chubby Checker–style. Next, pat all over: arms, legs, buttocks, chest, face, neck, and shoulders. Finally, shake your arms, legs, and your whole body if you can.

Whole-body exercises like these prior to doing ET can reduce tension, enhance your energy, and create a strong sense of presence. Some people dissociate when tuning in a trauma and these physical movements can help you to stay in the now rather than going into a dissociation trance.

Distancing

After tuning in and rating the SUD, visualize the traumatic event dimly and off in the distance while using an ET technique. This can also help to reduce any emotional reaction. Additionally you can picture the event upside down, in fast-forward or slow motion, from a bird's-eye view, in color or black and white, and so on. You can also change the sounds in various ways, such as making them quieter, distant, muffled, or by adding music.

Containing Emotional Reactions

Another way to prevent severe emotional reactions while tuning in and treating trauma is to use the Container Technique. This is a very simple process.

CONTAINER TECHNIQUE

Bring the trauma (or any aspect of it) to mind, rate the SUD level, and then imagine placing it in a container. The container can be anything—a box, a cylinder with a cover, and so on. Then quit thinking about the trauma and do the ET technique. Each time you complete a round of tapping or whatever procedure you're using, take a guess about the SUD level of the trauma or aspect in the container. After several rounds, your intuition may be that the SUD level is 0 or very low. At that time, take the scene out of the container and notice how you feel. Generally this works very well to reduce the SUD. If the SUD is not yet down to 0, put the trauma back into the container and do the treatment again. Keep going until the SUD is 1 or 0.

You can also put many aspects of the trauma or even several traumas in the container and then treat them in this manner.

Safe Space

At times, it's useful to create a "safe space" before trying to treat a trauma. One way to do this is to create an image in your mind that elicits a feeling of safety and security. This can be anything from a favorite room to an animal or person with whom you feel very safe. Bring this to mind and imagine it as vividly as you can while tapping the MET points: third eye (TE), under nose (UN), under bottom lip (UBL), upper chest (CH). Alternatively, you can use ESP to install the safe space. After you feel safe and comfortable, proceed to treat the trauma that you wish to resolve.

Take a Break

If you are not getting anywhere using a technique, rather than spinning your wheels and getting frustrated, take a break. Sometimes you are just not in the right mood to deal with a problem. At such times, it's better to be kind to yourself and do something you enjoy. The trauma will always be there to treat at another time.

Establishing Your Goal

While your obvious goal is to eliminate the trauma, it's generally a good idea to know not just where you are but also where you're heading. This is a matter of putting your outcome or future first and getting a firm handle on your health.

Future First

Often it is useful to create a future reference before treating the negative state of the trauma. To do this, you ask yourself this question: "After the trauma is resolved, what will be different?" Then write about that in detail. Focus on all the changes that would exist if you no longer suffered from the trauma: How will you feel, behave, sleep, talk, and so on? What will you believe that you don't believe now? After you get a fairly clear idea of what that would be, keep that in mind and do an effective technique for installing that future state. Consider using FOH, MET, or ESP. After the results are clearly in mind, treat the trauma.

Health First

Besides establishing your goals and orienting to them, it's a good idea to get into a state of health first. We've already covered several suggestions along these lines in this chapter. Think about how you feel when you're feeling your best. Clear your mind. Take some deep breaths. Drink some water or herbal tea. Go for a walk. Get into your emotional health and establish an anchor to give you access to this state. The anchor could be a visual image, an object to hold, a mantra or specific word, or perhaps specific music that helps you to maintain this state while doing ET for trauma.

Preventing Regression

After you eliminate the distress of a trauma, all you know for sure is that the distress is gone for the moment. Usually this is quite amazing, since up to now probably you have not been able to think about the traumatic event without feeling upset. Still the question remains: How long will the relief last? While the relief usually does last, here are a few additional things you can do to make sure that the trauma is gone for good:

Conviction

After you have resolved the trauma, it is often useful to ask, "How convinced am I that the trauma will remain resolved?" Then rate the level of certainty 0 to 10, with 10 indicating you are absolutely certain and 0 meaning you are totally uncertain. If you are within the 8 to 10 range, you're probably in good shape. If the certainty level is lower, you can often increase this by tapping on the back of your hand (BH) while internally telling yourself and picturing that the results will last. Just keep tapping BH and notice the level of certainty rise. You are aiming to be within the 8 to 10 range, and preferably 10.

Beliefs

A belief is a thought that something is true, even though you don't have absolute proof. A belief includes a feeling of conviction. When you have proof or knowledge that something is true, that's obviously different than a belief. Truth is fact; belief may be supported by facts, but it's still not fact. For example, you might believe that there's life on other planets, but since you don't have knowledge of that, you can't legitimately say that it's true. You just believe it.

Some beliefs are very useful, since they can guide our behavior and passage through life in positive ways. Other beliefs can limit and hurt us. If you believe that you are able to succeed in doing something, this increases the chances that you will succeed. If you believe that you will fail, guess what? Henry Ford said, "If you think you can do a thing or think you can't do a thing, you're right."

When you experience a traumatic event, you may draw a negative conclusion or make a negative decision about yourself, others, or certain situations; that decision constitutes a belief. Your intense fear at the time of the event is attached to your decision or conclusion, and this becomes a limiting belief that continues to play out in your life. Some examples of negative beliefs installed in trauma include a sense of being worthless, powerless, incapable, ruined, unlovable, evil, and so on. Sometimes these negative messages were delivered by another person at the time you were suffering the traumatic event. Whether delivered by you or someone else, these messages become firmly fixed or "imprinted" in your mind. They are basically posthypnotic suggestions that continue to exercise power over your life until you erase them.

Sometimes the limiting belief will change after you treat your trauma, but it's a good idea to figure out what your belief is and what you would prefer to believe instead. For example, if, as a result of the trauma, you believe that you are powerless, consider changing the belief to something like, "I'm strong and I survived." But how can you do this? Here's a technique for changing negative beliefs:

TECHNIQUE FOR CHANGING NEGATIVE BELIEFS

1. Tune in the negative belief.

2. Rate your level of conviction 0 to 10.

3. Correct reversal by tapping the little-finger side of your hand while saying three times, "Even though I have this negative belief, I deeply and completely accept myself."

4. Use an ET technique such as MET or one of the trauma techniques, such as energy tapping for highly complex trauma.

5. Continue with treatment until the level of conviction is 0 or very low.

6. Now think about your preferred belief.

7. Rate your level of conviction 0 to 10.

8. Tap between your little finger and ring finger on the back of your hand (BH) point while repeating this belief in your mind until the level of conviction is within the 8 to 10 range.

9. If the level of conviction doesn't increase adequately, consider other adjustments recommended in this chapter, such as correcting other reversals and energy disorganization (switching/neurologic disorganization).

10. You may need to repeat this treatment a few times over the next several days.

Forgiveness

After successfully treating a trauma, it is helpful, if possible, to forgive everyone and everything that caused or contributed to the trauma. This might be really hard to do in some cases, especially if someone did something awful to you. However, continuing to harbor anger, resentment, and hatred often prevents the trauma from being thoroughly resolved. Think of forgiveness as lightening your load. When you forgive, this does not mean that you condone what happened. It simply means that you are no longer willing to be upset about it in any way. So if you notice any emotions that are holding you back, tune in to the "unforgiveness" and remove it with MET. This issue is covered in more detail in chapter 7.

Personal and Professional Support

Sometimes it is difficult to treat yourself for a trauma or other results of trauma. In this case, you ought to seek out assistance. Here are a couple suggestions.

A Little Help from Your Friends

If you experience difficulty applying the ET techniques, get together with a friend or a group of friends and assist each other in going through the techniques. Often if someone is guiding you through the process, you'll find it easier to get results. Also, whether you're guiding someone or they're guiding you, it's obviously important to be supportive and nonjudgmental. It would not be wise to be pairing up like this if the process could stir up greater stress.

Help from a Therapist

Many therapists have skill with these techniques. So if you are unable to get results through self-help, consider consulting a therapist. You can also use these self-help techniques while seeing a good therapist, even if he or she is not trained in EP and ET. Also, appendix C of this book provides information about how you can locate therapists trained in these methods.

Now after you have eliminated trauma, depending on how traumatized you have been, the next order of business may be reconnecting to your life. The ideas and techniques covered in chapter 7 will assist you with this.

7

Reconnecting to and Empowering Your Life

Every moment of your life is infinitely creative and the universe is endlessly bountiful. Just put forth a clear enough request, and everything your heart desires must come to you.

—Mahatma Gandhi

Traumatic events can cause chronic traumatic stress, which I also call "trauma" in this book. However, your conscious memory of the event is not the same as the trauma itself. The conscious memory is certainly related to the trauma, but unconscious memory is the more significant source of traumatic stress. The unconscious memory is stored in your body other than where you consciously think and remember. This includes the fight-flight-freeze areas of your brain (limbic system), other cells, and your energy fields.

The techniques you have learned so far are effective for deactivating the unconscious body memory, balancing your energies, and relieving trauma. I hope that you have already experienced success with ET in ridding yourself of trauma. However, if you still have trauma to treat, please return to earlier chapters before (or after) reading this chapter and use these techniques to eliminate trauma. If self-treatment seems to be too stressful for you at this time, give yourself a break until you feel in a better state to do it. Using some of the techniques described in chapters 5 and 6 to help you reduce stress in general can prepare you to focus on eliminating trauma. Also use the techniques described in chapter 6 for preventing upset before specifically treating a trauma. And, if necessary, you always have the option of working with a therapist who has expertise in these effective techniques. In appendix C of this book, I offer you some recommendations for finding a qualified therapist.

Unhealthy Adaptations

Often it is enough to relieve the trauma, especially if the traumatic event happened recently, to make your life more livable. But sometimes eliminating trauma is only a part of what you need. When you live with trauma for a long time, you may adapt to it in unhealthy ways. Often these adaptations are mistaken solutions that create added burden in your life. Perhaps you turn to food, spending, alcohol, drugs, sex, or other reckless activities to distract you from distressing trauma symptoms. Maybe you experience worry, tension, headaches, panic attacks, or other emotional and behavior problems that may be subconscious attempts to protect yourself from imagined danger. As well intentioned as these strategies may be, they also create distress and unhappiness. Unfortunately, some victims of trauma also compulsively inflict trauma on others in a misguided attempt to no longer be the victim. All of these behaviors add trauma to trauma.

This chapter covers ways to further improve your life after you have eliminated trauma. This includes overcoming unhealthy adaptations, instilling gratitude, harnessing the power of intention and thought, building a firm sense of resources, and using these resources to resolve limitations brought on by trauma.

If traumatic events occurred early in your life, you may have experienced emotional and psychological arrest, since you did not get certain needs fulfilled. Early trauma can make it difficult to trust, to develop a sense of healthy independence, to accomplish goals, to have healthy, loving relationships, and so on. The emphasis in this chapter is on methods of resolving limitations created by trauma.

Also, at some level, trauma and trauma adaptation are maintained in thought. It is possible to learn to dismiss unhealthy thoughts and memories when they intrude and to positively apply this skill in other areas of your life. Partly this is accomplished by observing the thought or memory, seeing it as thought, and then not becoming attached to it as something that is real. After all, there is a difference between your thoughts and reality, although your thoughts are often reflections of something real.

This chapter goes into detail about how to accomplish this "dismissal" process in healthy ways.

Healthy Adaptations

Of course, not all adaptations to trauma are unhealthy, and with healthy adaptations the sting of trauma is significantly reduced and possibly eliminated. For example, if you learn something of importance as a result of suffering trauma, you may find ways to contribute to the welfare of others, essentially transforming the trauma into a resource. Some people make tremendously positive things happen after living with trauma for a time. You can make a significant contribution to society and the world, and as a result you get to move up the consciousness "food chain." Think of those who suffer rape, assault, or war trauma and then advocate for others who have suffered similar trauma. When you make a contribution in this way, you not only use your energies to help others and make the world a better place, but you also extinguish any feelings of powerlessness from the trauma and you reclaim your personal power. As a result of trauma in my life, I've come to more deeply understand the plight of others and how to help them. Even this book is a contribution as a result of my personal experience with trauma.

Personal Resilience

You might experience any number of symptoms after suffering a traumatic event. Most of the time people are resilient though. Very seldom do long-term adjustment problems or PTSD develop after such events. Initially you are shocked and may experience distressing symptoms, but these tend to wane within a short time, even without therapy. When that doesn't happen, however, there are effective treatments that can help you get back to health. We have covered many of these treatments in this book. Even if you choose professional treatment, it's important to understand that, at the core, you are healthy and treatment is essentially a way of helping you to get in touch with your innate health. The techniques covered in this chapter are geared to help you tap into your health.

Treatment and Evidence

Some of the treatment methods covered in this book have considerable empirical research support, and others do not. While you should look for approaches that are supported by research, not having research support does not necessarily mean that an approach is ineffective. All currently accepted treatment methods lacked research support early on. Initially, techniques are created from theory or intuition, or they are accidentally stumbled upon. Scientific research is only conducted after the developers have found the techniques to be effective with a number of people. Nevertheless, you ought to be choosy and take research, reason, and common sense into account when deciding on an approach to help you resolve a problem. Obviously you also ought to pay attention to your experience. If a technique works for you, it doesn't much matter if it lacks extensive scientific research support. Of course, some people might argue that something other than the technique accounts for the change, but that doesn't much matter either, since you are now feeling and functioning better. Although we're hungry for more research to confirm the benefits of ET, it already has considerable research support. And there are many therapists who are highly skilled in this approach and apply it daily to help their clients overcome trauma and other psychological problems.

You can effectively treat addictions, phobias, depression, panic attacks, dissociation, and many other consequences of and adaptations to traumatic events with the techniques covered in this book, although the assistance of a qualified therapist is often helpful. If a technique tailored to a specific issue is needed, consult my book *Energy Tapping* for additional help. But generally you can use one of the ET techniques covered in chapter 5, especially energy tapping for highly complex trauma, the Midline Energy Treatment (MET), and the Eight-Step Process (ESP). However, regardless of the technique you choose, the basic formula remains the same:

1. Bring the problem to mind.

2. Notice and rate your subjective units of discomfort (SUD) 0 to 10.

3. Correct for switching and reversal, if necessary.

4. Follow the ET process until the discomfort is gone.

5. Enhance your results further by using techniques and understandings covered in this chapter.

Extraordinary Energies

The techniques covered so far help you to tune in a disturbing memory or other issue and deactivate it by stimulating your body in specific ways. These techniques, however, are only one way to regain your health. Another way is to access deeper feelings, which will balance your energy quickly and profoundly. These deeper feelings are beyond basic emotions such as anger, grief, jealousy, modesty, sympathy, excitement, and jubilance. Both positive and negative emotions are frenetic; deeper feelings have a calm quality. Deeper feelings include love, compassion, enthusiasm, awe, joy, humility, resolve, admiration, serenity, and gratitude. We'll look more closely at two of these—compassion and gratitude—a little later in this chapter.

At the core of emotions and deeper feelings is thought, although each of these sensations involves a different thinking process—a thinking process that occurs throughout your body, from your head to your heart to your toes. This is more than simply words or pictures in your head, although these are certainly thought as well. Deeper feelings are hardwired, and they seem to automatically come to the surface when you quiet your mind. This often happens while taking a soothing shower or bath, on a relaxing vacation, walking on a beach, listening to a gentle rain, or engaging in other activities that you enjoy.

These deeper feelings offer many benefits. One study demonstrated a significant improvement in the immune systems of subjects who simply watched a film of Mother Teresa being caring and compassionate with poor people in the streets of Calcutta (McClelland and Kirshnit 1988). Watching the film helped the viewers to get in touch with feelings of compassion and caring, which boosted their immune systems. Another experiment showed that a few minutes of anger significantly suppresses your immune system, while a few minutes of care and compassion greatly enhance it (Rein, Atkinson, and McCraty 1995). In addition, people who kept gratitude journals exercised regularly, had fewer physical symptoms, felt better about their lives, and were more optimistic than those who recorded hassles or neutral life events in their journals (Emmons and McCullough 2003, 2004). So deeper feelings like compassion and gratitude are not only important for your relationships and happiness, they are also essential for your health. So it makes good sense to get in touch with compassion and gratitude often. Let's take a closer look at these deeper feelings.

Compassion

One of the most succinct compassion statements was delivered by Jesus of Nazareth at the Sermon on the Mount when he said, "Blessed are the merciful, for they shall obtain mercy" (Matthew 5:7). Similarly, Christian theologian Matthew Fox stated, "Compassion is not sentiment but is making justice and doing works of mercy … a flow and overflow of the fullest human and divine energies." The Dalai Lama offered a strategy for actualizing compassion when he said, "Compassion can be put into practice if one recognizes the fact that every human being is a member of humanity and the human family regardless of differences in religion, culture, color, and creed." And famed conductor and cellist Pablo Casals emphasized, "The capacity to care is the thing which gives life its deepest significance."

Compassion and sympathy are distinct. Compassion is a deep feeling of love for another in their plight. Compassion feels good; there is no pain associated with it.

While sympathy can certainly be a good thing, it is an emotion that often hurts. When you feel sympathy, you identify with and hurt for and with the suffering person. With compassion you care in a deeper, loving way. You understand and your heart reaches out to help the other, whether human or any other life-form. You can even have compassion for inanimate objects. While "sympathy fatigue" occurs often among people whose efforts to help produce no positive results, "compassion fatigue" is not possible, since true compassion is always positively energizing. So now it's time for some compassion. Sit back and try the following exercise.

COMPASSION EXERCISE

1. Get in touch with the feeling of compassion now. What does it feel like? Where do you feel compassion in your body? What does it move you to do? Bring to mind a person, animal, or thing that needs your compassion. If you feel pain while doing this process, perhaps it is sympathy or agony you feel. Compassion involves love and understanding.

2. Rate the level of compassion that you are feeling on a scale of 0 to 10, with 10 being the highest level. Also see if you can intensify the feeling. How do you accomplish this?

3. Tap on the back of hand (BH) point between your little finger and ring finger while focusing on the feeling of compassion. This can increase the intensity of the feeling. Again notice where you feel compassion.

4. Do acts of loving-kindness and compassion as soon as you can. It is not enough to just feel compassion. Compassion requires action in the direction that your *compass*-ion points.

5. Regularly recall this experience and repeat the Compassion Exercise.

Gratitude

The Greek philosopher Epictetus said, "He is a wise man who does not grieve for the things which he has not, but rejoices for those which he has." The Roman philosopher and politician Cicero wrote, "Gratitude is not only the greatest of virtues, but the parent of all the others." And the Christian mystic Meister Eckhart said, "If the only prayer you said in your whole life was 'thank you,' that would suffice."

It's interesting that the linguistic roots of the word "gratitude" include words such as "openly praise" and "grace." Gratitude is not simply an emotion like excitement. Excitement is frenetic, while gratitude is a calm and glowing state. Get in touch with gratitude now and notice how it feels. It's a wonderful feeling, isn't it? Gratitude is a deeper spiritual feeling and is related to love. You can think of love as light shining through a prism, revealing the spectrum of the various colors of gratitude, joy, compassion, and hope. "Transduction" is the process of converting one type of energy to another. All of these deeper feelings are transduced from the energy of love.

Forgiveness is an important ingredient of healing. Yet perceiving that you have been hurt or mistreated generally precedes forgiveness. Usually lack of forgiveness precedes forgiveness. However, the prerequisite of being hurt or offended is not necessary to have gratitude. You can be grateful any time you set your mind and heart to it. And it's important to activate gratitude often. When you are grateful, your energies are positively harmonized and this cultivates serenity, tranquility, calm, and enhanced health. Indeed, gratitude is an energy and consciousness vibration that communicates the message of health.

Look around and listen. Many people spend a lot of time being upset. "Things aren't going right!" "People should treat me better!" "I can't stand it!" "It's awful!" "I'm worried about ..." By focusing on the negative, your life energy is disrupted with all the accompanying chemical imbalance, compromised immunity, ill health, unhappiness, poor relationships, self-sabotage, and so on.

An alternative is to access gratitude and send it throughout your body, throughout your being, throughout your relationships with people and things. Gratitude gives a better slant on life, and through gratitude you give life a better slant. You do not need to resolve negatives before accessing gratitude; you can simply calm your mind and create gratitude. Actually, gratitude and other positive feelings often show up shortly after tapping away trauma and other negative thoughts and emotions. To a large extent, this is a function of cleaning and clearing your mind of disturbing thoughts and memories. The serenity and creativity experienced on a relaxing vacation is not simply due to the change of environment; it's primarily the result of relaxing your mind. Thus health must be your innate default setting.

No doubt there are times when it is exceptionally difficult to feel gratitude. Everything seems to be going wrong and it's easy to get caught up in stress and distress. The problem is that if you go with emotions such as anger, resentment, jealousy, anxiety, and all the other versions of fear, you're apt to get more of the same—more things will go wrong. So shifting to gratitude will not only make you feel a whole lot better, but it also increases the chances that you'll get more of what you truly want and deserve.

Okay, how do we create or get in touch with gratitude? Basically you just do it. Having a technique is not absolutely necessary to create gratitude, but techniques are like training wheels that can help you to deepen gratitude in your life. So as you read through the following Gratitude Exercise, please do it. You and I will be forever grateful if you do!

GRATITUDE EXERCISE

1.   First, quiet your mind and create a safe space. Place the palm of one hand at the center of your chest and put your focus there. Imagine being in a comfortable scene, such as resting on a hill and looking down at a valley, or walking on a beach and listening to the gentle splashing waves, or whatever you prefer. If you're caught up in a negative state, understand that emotion is basically a reflection of your current state of psychological functioning. Essentially clear your mind by understanding that you create your experience in thought. Although thoughts automatically pass through your mind, the activity of thinking is yours. You're the thinker. Don't try to block out thoughts, just let them come and go without being attached to them.

2.   After calming your mind, picture something, someone, or an incident that calls to mind gratitude. Recall a time when you felt gratitude, or get in touch with how gratitude feels. Perhaps picture someone you know who is really good at gratitude and imagine what that is like.

3.   Associate with their experience—that is, step into it. Notice how you smile and walk and move when you're in gratitude, when gratitude is in you. Don't just do this in imagery; actually engage in it physically. Your feeling state has certain bodily patterns. Notice the way you hold your body, position your face, and gesture when you feel gratitude. What is your tone of voice when you feel gratitude? Create these bodily patterns now!

4.   Then let gratitude blossom and radiate. Let it grow by really tuning in to it. Picture or think about this deeper feeling in detail. The incident, person, or thing might be simple or profound. You might think about someone or something you love. You might think about the wonders of the universe. You might focus on all the benefits you receive from the various parts of your body: your eyes, ears, nose, mouth, legs, arms, hands, and feet. Really appreciate them!

5.   You can also get to gratitude by thinking about the gifts life has given you— the wonderful aroma of Grandmother's hot apple pie, your first bicycle, your first doll. Locate those things that warm your gratitude hearth.

6.   After getting in touch with gratitude and holding it in your mind and heart, strengthen it by tapping, rubbing, or holding the third eye (TE) point on your forehead while continuing to hold your other hand at the center of your

chest. Hold this position for ten to twenty seconds, or until you feel that the energy connection has been significantly strengthened. You might like to calculate subjective units of gratitude (SUG), with 10 being the height of gratitude. Doing this technique with several thoughts of gratitude is useful. Frequently, thinking about one experience will often call others to mind automatically. Stack them up. By doing this, you create an energetic anchor that gives you access to gratitude. In the future, you can simply hold this energetic anchor position to get in touch with gratitude.

7. Once you have developed and strengthened gratitude in this way, locate a memory of an event in your life that can benefit from the healing energies of gratitude. Re-create the event vividly and bathe it in gratitude. Observe as the subjective units of discomfort (SUD) descend and the SUG rises.

Gratitude Anchors

While walking along the north bank of Lake Zwischenahn in northern Germany in 2006, I found a small piece of deep-brown flint. Similar to when I had found a four-leaf clover several years earlier, I felt grateful for finding the stone. I was teaching an EP course in the area, so I gathered many more interesting looking stones to give to the participants. Remember collecting lucky stones as a child? A lucky stone is white. Well, these are gratitude stones and they can be any color you like. The nice thing about a gratitude stone is that you can carry it in your pocket or purse and it reminds you to be grateful. Find your own personal gratitude stone today and carry it with you! You'll know your gratitude stone when you see it. Of course, instead of a stone you can choose any object that prompts gratitude for you—a polished piece of wood, a button, a baby Buddha, a plastic angel, a cross, and so on. These objects work like anchors that help you to hold gratitude in place.

Regardless of how you get in touch with gratitude, it is right there within the core of your being. You have the ability to create a wide array of states and behaviors. While you always have the ability to spend time in negative states like regret, resentment, jealousy, and guilt, you also have the option of creating gratitude anytime you choose. You create your experience through the use of your mind, your thoughts, your behaviors, and your energy. And since you are conscious, you get to experience the detriment or benefit of your thoughts, emotions, and feelings. Choose wisely!

Your Best Possible Self

In the 1950s, psychologist Dr. George A. Kelly explored the benefits of helping his clients to act like their ideal selves (Kelly 1955). He assumed that personality is a function of behavior and that by acting differently in a variety of situations, you can actually alter your beliefs and constructs about yourself and thus transform your personality for the better. His method was called *fixed role therapy* and was influenced by the ideas of German philosopher Hans Vaihinger. Vaihinger's *Philosophy of As If* emphasizes that your perception of reality is based on assumptions or beliefs, and that you do not know how things ultimately "really" are. This applies to science as well as everyday life, which suggests that much of who you think you are (your personality) is made up. In a sense, you live in a constructed model of the world and yourself. While this may sound negative, in many ways this is a positive postmodern view that highlights freedom, since you are able to construct a reality of your choosing.

Kelly treated several hundred people with fixed role therapy and found that it helped to significantly loosen their constructs and beliefs about themselves. He worked with them to design a detailed script of how they would rather be—not the complete opposite of themselves but rather more in the direction of their best selves. They would have some sessions where the client would role-play the part. Kelly would also give assignments to play the new role around strangers as well as acquaintances, friends, and family. The experiment would take place over a two-week period. Although these practices did not cause an ongoing dramatic change in the personalities of the clients, it did become clear that if you have a negative and limiting view of yourself and you experience even a brief shift of self-perception, this can pave the way for profound positive change.

In a similar vein, researchers explored the benefits of writing about your *best possible self* (BPS) with a group of college students. They found that this exercise resulted in a significant increase in positive emotions and feelings (Sheldon and Lyubomirsky 2006). However, it's important to note that long-term benefits required persistence. Obviously you can't expect feelings of happiness to last without reinforcement. The study also compared the BPS exercise with gratitude journaling (counting your blessings) and paying attention to and journaling about the details of your life. All three approaches resulted in a reduction in negative emotions, although BPS journaling produced more positive emotions and feelings.

BEST POSSIBLE SELF (BPS) EXERCISE

Your assignment, should you choose to accept it, is to maintain a BPS journal over the next six weeks to help you get in touch with those aspects of yourself that you would like to actualize. Here are some guidelines:

1. Before you start, rate your general level of happiness (LOH) on a scale of 0 to 10, with 10 being the highest level.

2. Each day before you write in your journal, record your LOH so that you'll have a measure of your progress.

3. Write about your BPS for no more than five minutes.

4. Next, energetically reinforce your BPS for one minute by tapping on the MET treatment points while visualizing your BPS. The MET treatment points are as follows: third-eye point on your forehead between your eyebrows (TE), under nose (UN), under bottom lip (UBL), center of upper chest (CH).

5. In addition to writing in your journal, actualize elements of your BPS in your behavior. Generally it is not enough to simply imagine your BPS. It's most effective to make it happen in your everyday life.

6. After six weeks, write in your journal about your progress. Compare the BPS Exercise with other exercises we have covered in this chapter.

7. From now on, use the exercise or hybrid that suits you best. Write in your journal once a week (or more often if you prefer).

Having a BPS anchor can help you to stay the course. This can be a stone, a small piece of wood, a button, a baby Buddha, a plastic angel, a cross, or something else that means a lot to you. These objects work like anchors that remind you to manifest your BPS.

Healing Energy Light Process (HELP)

The Healing Energy Light Process (HELP) is a technique that can assist you in harnessing the power of your intention to achieve whatever outcomes you have in mind. It integrates some ET techniques you've already learned with some others not previously covered in this book. In the place of tapping on meridian acupoints, you will touch the ET points, since touching is less likely to interrupt the meditative experience that is central to HELP. Be mindful of thoughts as they come and go without getting caught up in them. This is a relaxing process that corrects energy disorganization and reversal. As you will discover, it is also a spiritually oriented process. HELP is beneficial in the treatment of many psychological, relationship, and even some physical problems, including chronic pain.

A gentleman in his midforties came to see me because of depression related to the fact that his twenty-year-old daughter would have nothing to do with him. In the early days of his separation from her mother, she would visit with him, but that stopped sometime during early adolescence. He regularly tried to contact her—sending letters and cards, calling her by phone, giving presents on her birthday and at Christmas, and so on. While she was in college, he attempted to visit her at the dormitory several times, but she would not receive him. To say the least, he was crushed.

We used HELP to assist him in resolving the distress about his daughter. After the initial treatment he felt much better, more at peace about his daughter and feeling that eventually things would work out for them. Perhaps it is a coincidence, but when I saw him in follow-up two weeks later, he reported that after all these years of alienation, his daughter spontaneously contacted him and indicated a desire to see him. That was nearly two years ago and their relationship is good. They see each other regularly and the previous falling out is a thing of the past.

Perhaps it is not a coincidence at all. Perhaps this effect is consistent with the positive results frequently found with prayer and distant healing. Consciousness and energy are interrelated and when you resolve a relationship problem within yourself, this causes the energy to resonate and touch the other person in a positive way, even at a distance.

So enough with the discussion. It's time for you to give HELP a try. So sit back and give yourself a little break from reading and do the following exercise.

HELP EXERCISE

1. Hold in mind the goal or purpose for which you are doing HELP. For example, goals might include any desirable outcome, such as overcoming depression, increasing self-confidence and comfort in social situations, resolving panic attacks, eliminating migraines, improving your relationships, and so on.

2. Correct a possible reversal by tapping continually on the little-finger side of your hand (SH) or rubbing the sore spot (SS) on the left side of your chest while saying or thinking three times, "Even if I'm not aligned with my goal, I deeply and completely accept myself, and I choose to be aligned with this goal."

3. Do the Hook-Up Technique: Cross your left ankle over your right. Hold your hands out in front of you, arms extended, with palms facing. Then turn your hands over so your thumbs point down and the back of the hands are touching. Raise your right hand up and over your left hand, and interlock

the fingers. Turn your hands in and up so that your hands are resting on your chest under your chin.

4. Place the tip of your tongue at the roof of your mouth behind your teeth. Take some slow, deep diaphragmatic breaths in through your nose. Close your eyes and attend to your steady, slow breathing. Also sense that the breath is coming in through the bottom of your feet all the way up through your body. Comfortably hold in mind your intention while doing this.

5. Become aware that there is a perpetual healing light shining down onto your head. This light is a color of your choosing, a color that you associate with healing. This light comes in through the top of your head as you are breathing and then travels throughout your body, vibrating into every cell, every fiber of your body: from the top of your head all the way down your shoulders, into your chest and stomach, into your legs and arms, into your feet and hands. Simply continue to experience this for a little while, perhaps a minute or two. Comfortably hold in mind your intention while doing this.

6. Next, unlock your fingers, arms, and legs. Set your feet flat on the floor, and place your fingertips in a pyramid-like position, the fingertips of the left hand touching the fingertips of your right hand. Your palms are not touching. While you maintain this position, continue to keep the tip of your tongue at the roof of your mouth and to breathe slowly and steadily. Continue to sense the perpetual light glowing throughout your body and giving power to your intention to achieve your goal. As you breathe, continue to notice the breath coming in through the bottom of your feet. Maintain this position for perhaps a minute or two. Comfortably hold in mind your intention.

7. Discontinue this pyramid position, and just notice how you feel. Next, rest one hand on your lap and place the index and middle fingers of the other hand on your forehead slightly above and between your eyebrows (the third-eye point). Just lightly place your fingers there. Take in a deep breath from your diaphragm and then slowly exhale. If you are experiencing any tension or discomfort of any kind, imagine or think that the discomfort is dissipating. Also think or say this phrase: "Any remaining aspects of this problem are being eliminated from my whole being, from my body, mind, and soul."

8. Place the same two fingers lightly under your nose. Take in a deep breath from your diaphragm and then slowly exhale while thinking or saying, "Any remaining aspects of this problem are being eliminated from my whole being, from my body, mind, and soul." Exhale completely and relax.

9. Place the same two fingers under your bottom lip and take a diaphragmatic breath in and slowly exhale while thinking or saying, "Any remaining aspects

of this problem are being eliminated from my whole being, from my body, mind, and soul." Exhale and relax.

10. Place the fingertips of one hand at the upper section of your chest and rest your other hand on your lap. You can slowly thump on your chest if you prefer. Take a slow deep breath in and slowly exhale while thinking or saying, "Any remaining aspects of this problem are being eliminated from my whole being, from my body, mind, and soul." Exhale and relax.

11. Place the palm of one of your hands at the center of your chest over your heart and get in touch with the feeling of love, appreciation, or gratitude. Do this in any way that suits you best. Perhaps thinking about your love or gratitude for a particular person, an animal, the earth, or a special toy can facilitate this process. Center that feeling in the area immediately around your heart and focus on energy flowing to fulfill your intention. You might use a phrase to facilitate this. For example, "I am sending healing love to fulfill this intention," or "Healing love, appreciation, and gratitude are giving energy to this intention."

12. Finally, return your awareness to your surroundings and give yourself some time to reorient. Reconsider the issue for which you did this process. Insights may occur to you immediately after completing the process or later on. Consider repeating HELP several times over the next few weeks to powerfully activate your intention.

The Healing Unified Self

Trauma that occurs early in life can interfere with healthy psychological development. For example, it is during the first couple years of life that you develop your sense of trust. If your parents are responsive to your needs when you are hungry, wet, tired, or in pain, you develop a sense of basic trust. You know that you can count on them and by implication you develop trust in the world. If your parents are not able to respond appropriately to your needs, you may develop a sense of basic mistrust. Resolving trauma by using techniques from this book can help you to eliminate and overcome interruptions in your psychological development.

Yet sometimes it is not enough to eliminate trauma, and sometimes traumatic events per se were not even factors in arresting your emotional development. For example, while growing up in a family atmosphere that did not sufficiently nurture and protect you is not necessarily traumatic in the general sense, it is significantly depriving. Such a situation can prevent you from developing trust, an appropriate autonomy, and from being able to appropriately love, nurture, and protect others.

Did you ever wonder what it would be like if you could go back in time and alter negative events from the past in healthier ways? If you did not experience adequate nurturance, protection, and guidance during your early years, what if instead you were showered with healthy love, nurturance, and protection? Well, you'd be quite different, wouldn't you? Your personality is formed as a result of a bit of heredity combined with lots of input from the environment. You take in stimuli from the world around you (people, places, things, and events) and incorporate this into yourself (thoughts, beliefs, emotional reactions, behaviors) without even knowing that you're doing it. In a sense, you're not doing it. Instead the environment is doing it to you. Traumatic stress as a result of traumatic events is just a striking example of what happens to you all the time in different ways. Something from the outside goes inside, attaches itself to your life, and "lives" a life of its own—like a virus. It is definitely possible to eliminate these mental viruses by applying the techniques covered so far in addition to the Unified Self Process™ Exercise below.

Unified Self Process (USP)

The Unified Self Process involves getting in touch with the energies and resources of nurturance, protection, and your spiritual core, helping to transform negative memories of events and periods of past neglect when important needs were not fulfilled. This process can help resolve trauma and also create a deeper sense of security, trust, and responsibility. Although the assistance of a therapist is often needed, here the process is described in some detail for self use.

UNIFIED SELF PROCESS (USP) EXERCISE

1. Identify an event or a period of time in your childhood that interfered with your development. It could be ongoing unavailability of a parent, being deprived in some way, not being accepted by peers, or any number of other things. Think about the younger you back there in a situation representative of this trauma and/or neglect. If you cannot recall a specific event or scene, think of the time period and simply create a representation. This might be a picture of the younger you appearing afraid or distressed. And as you recall this representation, rate the SUD 0 to 10.

2. Set that situation aside, and take several deep breaths and relax. Then take another deep breath and allow yourself to drift back in time. Think of this as a time before time: a time when you were pure energy … pure spirit … peaceful … before thought … before limitations … all possibility … pure essence … pure being … innocence … love. It's not important that you actively think about how to do this. Just let your inner self and inner wisdom take you to that place. It is by your consideration alone that you can access this resource. And your body and mind know just how to connect with your soul.

3. Place two fingers of one hand between your eyebrows and slightly above your nose at the third-eye point. Tap there to strengthen this resource. Keep tapping until you feel a strong connection with this spiritual resource—until you feel that the strength of the resource is within the 8 to 10 range, with 10 being the positive end of the scale. Also create a notion or image of this resource. It might be a colorful light or whatever you prefer.

4. Move somewhat forward in time and get in touch with each of the following resources in you one at a time. Get in touch with the first resource before moving on to the next and so on. Access the resource by recalling a time when you experienced it in relationship to someone else, an animal, or an object. If you cannot locate a memory, create the state by imagining or thinking about the behavior of someone who does the behavior. Each time you access a resource, tap on the back of hand (BH) point of your left hand to strengthen it. Keep tapping until you feel that the resource is within the 8 to 10 range on a 10-point scale. Here are the resources: unconditionally loving … understanding … empathetic … kindhearted … gentle … warm … tender … accepting … approving … connected … relating … patient … encouraging. Also create a notion or image of these resources. It might be a colorful light or whatever you prefer.

5. Move even slightly more forward in time and get in touch with each of these resources in you one at a time. Get in touch with the first resource before moving on to the next and so on. Access the resource by recalling a time when you experienced it in relationship to someone else, an animal, or an object. If you cannot locate a memory, create the state by imagining or thinking about the behavior of someone who does the behavior. Each time you access a resource, tap on the back of hand (BH) point of your right hand to strengthen it. Keep tapping until you feel that the resource is within the 8 to 10 range on a 10-point scale. Here are the resources: able to maintain healthy limits and boundaries … dependable … reliable … confident … autonomous … decisive … active … tenacious … brave … strong … firm

... logical ... protective. Your body and mind know just how to connect with all of this in you. Also create a notion or image of these resources. It might be a colorful light or whatever you prefer.

6. Bring all of these resources together into a single unified self—and notice how you feel and anything else you experience. You might like to give this unified self a personal name.

7. Attend to your feelings and images involved in the unified self while holding the unified-self pose by placing one hand at the center of your chest and another hand on your forehead to anchor this resource state. When this state is strengthened, hold this position for about a minute and then discontinue this pose.

8. Think again about the representative event or a period of time in your childhood that interfered with your development. Think about the younger you back there in a situation representative of this trauma and/or neglect. And as you recall this, again rate the SUD 0 to 10.

9. Resume the unified-self pose (see #7 above) and see/feel your inner child having his/her needs fulfilled by the unified self. Your unified self is able to nurture, protect, and teach your younger self. Reconfigure the experience. Transform the events and situation in ways that are most pleasing and supportive of a healthy you. As you hold the unified-self pose, you will notice that it takes some time to experience your unified self in that situation. As soon as you are there in this new way, linger for a few moments, and then stop the pose and move around.

10. Repeat the last step an additional ten times. With each repetition, notice that the time it takes to dissolve the negativity of the representative experience lessens. The goal is to make it automatic.

11. Reevaluate the formative event. Is the SUD reduced? Do you see the event or time period differently now?

Obviously, this exercise cannot change the past as it occurred, although it can change the past as it is represented in your psyche, which is the way you see and experience your past. Sometimes it is necessary to do USP many times, reinforcing the positive resources. Each time you do this, you alter the memory and your experience about that time in your life. You are essentially re-parenting yourself and this can promote positive growth.

Thought Consciousness

Principles are basic components that are sometimes referred to as rules or laws. For example, in mathematics there are four basic principles or operations: addition, subtraction, multiplication, and division. All of mathematics uses these principles. However, in a sense there is only one fundamental principle, and that is addition. It is the basis of the other three principles. Multiplication is accelerated addition. Division is accelerated subtraction. And subtraction is addition in reverse.

Similarly, there are four basic principles involved in your psychological reality or experience, although they can all be reduced to the first principle. What follows may seem complex, but it's important to understand.

The first principle is energy, which is the fundamental fabric of everything that exists in our "material" world. Everything is made of energy, which comes together in different arrangements that are called mass or matter. Matter includes trees, rocks, cars, boats, golf balls, and even your body. There are different types of energy, including atomic energy, electricity, kinetic (motion) energy, and more. All types of energy involve the capacity for work or accomplishment. Without energy, things would just lazily lie around all day doing nothing. However, if you looked really close, you'd also see that there's energy involved in maintaining the form of the things that are just lying around. You know: the activity of atoms and molecules that comprise those things. And when you get down to it, all of the "parts" of atoms—electrons, neutrons, and protons—are simply vibrating energy waves, not solid matter at all. It's amazing how everything is essentially made from vibrating little waves, which are practically nothing!

The second principle is mind, which is the intelligence principle. You have a personal mind and you also share in Universal Mind, which is the intelligence principle throughout nature and the universe. This principle accounts for the laws of physics, chemistry, biology, psychology, and mathematics. Mind is formless energy and the capacity for form. Mind is the intelligence energy or power from which and within which thought occurs. No mind = no thought.

So the third principle is thought. Thought is mind energy in a specific form—such as the thought of a mountain, a person, a tree, a golf ball in the rough, or an abstract idea. Thought is physical (neurons or nerve cells), chemical (neurochemicals like serotonin and adrenaline), and, more fundamentally, electrical (or energy). Even when you are observing something external to yourself, such as a tree, it's practically impossible to separate what's outside from your thoughts. For example, even though you see the tree as external, you still have the thought that it is a tree and the word "tree" is a symbol (or thought) about this life-form. Also, you have all sorts of associations (other thoughts) about the tree and trees. For instance, when I was a young boy we had an apple tree in our backyard that I climbed with friends. We also had a cherry tree that just started to produce fruit around the time we moved to another house. Thought stems from mind, and there are two kinds of thought processes. One is analytical and methodical; the other is inspirational and creative. Analytical thought is effortful, and inspirational thought is a relaxed flow.

And the fourth principle is consciousness, which is your ability to be aware of external events (like the words you are reading on this page) and to experience your thoughts (like the thought of biting into a bitter lemon or a sour apple). Consciousness is understanding and reflective. When you have a thought, you have a level of awareness about the thought. That awareness includes a physical sensation, such as a reaction in your body, an emotion, or a feeling. Sometimes your awareness is at a very low level and you do not perceive that your thoughts account for your experience. And at other times, you are highly aware that your experience is a function of your thoughts. Through consciousness of thought, you are able to choose your reality and to exercise a degree of freedom.

So why should you consider these principles, and how are they important in helping you to reconnect to and empower your life? Knowing that your experience is largely created through thought energy is quite different from "thinking" that your experience is simply created from the outside and not a matter of choice. Even though the structures in your personal mind have a lot to do with input from your environment, you are still the thinker. Thoughts bubble to the surface of your mind and then you can delve into them (think about them) or let them go. You have tens of thousands of thoughts every day, so you are quite proficient at dismissing them. This has relevance to trauma and to your life as a whole as we will see below.

Navigating Your Experience: Mental Martial Art

I used to experience depressed feelings that would last for many days at a time. During these periods, I would feel empty and preoccupied with painful memories, anger and guilt feelings, disconnection from others, loneliness, and shame. Of course I didn't feel very good about myself. Then the gloom would pass and once again I would feel better. My mind would be more at ease and I would feel positive, connected with others, hopeful, and grateful.

One day I awoke feeling depressed and it occurred to me that what was bothering me didn't bother me the day before even though nothing had changed. In a flash, it became obvious to me that my thoughts were brought on by my energy or mood, and that my thoughts in turn were reinforcing this very feeling. It was a vicious cycle! Intellectually I had "learned" about this before, but for the first time I had a deep understanding of this in the moment.

It occurred to me that the more thinking or analyzing I did about my state, the more I got stuck in it. If I obsessed and ruminated about what was going on with me, this just kept me in the dismal state. And I also noticed that if I tried to push my thoughts and thinking away, it would just snap back with a vengeance. So I decided to apply what I call "mental martial art." A basic principle of the martial arts is that you utilize the aggressor's force and turn it against him. In mental martial art, you don't fight with your upsetting thoughts. You don't obsess about them. You don't try to force the thoughts away. You don't even try to replace negative thoughts with positive ones. In mental martial art, you recognize the thoughts as thoughts, and then you watch them go on their way. You simply observe: This is a thought. This is a feeling.

Interestingly, as soon as I understood this—as soon as I recognized this blind spot in my experience—it became a lot easier to not take my thoughts so seriously. I felt curious as I watched my thoughts, my feelings, and their connection to each other. And I had faith that if I simply quit feeding the thoughts, my energy would shift in a better direction. And that's exactly what happened within a reasonably short period of time. Before I knew it, my energy was better and my mood was positive.

The basic insight is this: your psychological experience is a function of your thoughts. This is true regardless of the accuracy of the thought and even if the thought is about something real. You feel "good" or "bad" because of the quality of your thought and the quality of your thinking. Generally, gratitude, love, hope, and joy are reflections of high-quality thought and high-quality thinking. Despair, hatred, depression, fear, hopelessness, rage, anger, guilt, jealousy, and other negative emotions and states are frequently reflections of low-quality thought and thinking. Of course, there can be value in certain negative emotions, like anger, fear, and jealousy, but usually a little bit goes a long way and too much of it tears you down.

When your energy is out of balance and your mood is low, usually all you need to do is get out of the way and your energy and mood will rise again. Life has its ups and downs, and so does your energy state. The weather changes, the seasons come and go, life has its cycles, and so do your energy states and moods. By clearing your mind when you are in a negative energy state, your energy can shift in a healthy direction and then living becomes easier again. Sometimes this shift occurs quickly and sometimes it takes time, but it won't happen very well or at all if you continue to be seduced by negative thoughts. Also, it's important to understand that your energy state and mood can be affected by fatigue, hunger, certain foods and substances, and your physical health. So paying attention to these factors is also essential to your psychological health.

Here's a chart that illustrates the characteristics of high and low energy:

HIGH ENERGY	LOW ENERGY
High Mood	Low Mood
Balanced	Imbalanced
Positive Thoughts	Negative Thoughts
Positive Emotions and Feelings	Negative Emotions
Feelings of Security	Feelings of Insecurity
Relaxed	Tense
Creative Inspirations	Obsessive Thinking
Healthy Functioning	Unhealthy Functioning

All of the techniques covered in this chapter and in chapter 6 balance your energy system to neutralize negative thoughts and negative emotions, and to instill positive thoughts and positive emotions. However, it is also possible to recognize that you consciously and unconsciously create your experience via thought. Trauma is stored in memory, which is essentially thought. Trauma reviewing is the process by which you inadvertently feed the trauma and keep it alive. Being aware of thoughts that produce negative emotional states and realizing that you are the thinker makes it easier to let go of the thoughts and return to energetic balance and healthy psychological functioning.

The techniques covered in this book can be thought of as training wheels for higher consciousness. As you alleviate the negative emotion attached to the traumatic memory through using these techniques, your emotional state shifts for the better and it becomes easier to see that the source of your distress was contaminated thought. As you continue to use these techniques, you will find that you need them less and less, since you will have greater command of your thoughts and your thinking process. Notice that as you clear your mind of negative thoughts and emotions, your thought process becomes more relaxed, effortless, creative, intuitive, and healthy. Naturally your energy and mood rise. You're experiencing what we call peace of mind.

8

Beginnings

We shall begin in exploration, and the end of all our exploring will be to return to the place where we started and know it for the first time.

—T. S. Eliot

We've explored trauma and its effects, considering it in terms of traumatic events, traumatic memories and thoughts, behavior, brain functioning, biochemistry, and bio-energy. And we've looked at customary and alternative treatments, with special focus on energetic approaches to healing trauma. Additionally, we've looked at how you can apply a variety of techniques and concepts to eliminate trauma and to improve the quality of your life. Although one or two ET techniques could have been the exclusive focus of this book, more options increase your chances of success. You've been offered an abundant array of techniques with which to help yourself and others. Choose what works best for you and design your pathways to health and happiness.

These techniques are unusual and you may find that it takes some convincing to get others to try them. Of course, after discovering the effectiveness of these techniques, skepticism becomes irrelevant. Yet don't be surprised if some people apply the techniques, feel better, and remain unconvinced. Well, be patient and let people have their skepticism. But encourage them to use the techniques, which you can best accomplish by example. By employing these methods to improve your own life, others will see that ET really works, even if the methods do seem unusual and too simple to be true. In a short time, this approach will not be so unusual, since it is already spreading worldwide.

Now, even though the term ET has been used throughout this book, a variety of techniques have been introduced. Energy psychology (EP) is the general theory used to understand psychological functioning as involving energy fields. And energy tapping (ET) is the technique of stimulating your body to balance your energy system and resolve psychological problems like trauma. Bodily stimulation includes tapping on meridian points, specific breathing patterns, holding your hands at various locations on your body, moving in certain ways, and even some types of visualization. You've learned that you can resolve trauma with these and related techniques and also through increasing your awareness of thought. You've also learned that these techniques and concepts are not limited to removing trauma, but they can also be used to treat a variety of problems and to assist you in enhancing the quality of your life.

Freedom and Determinism

It's interesting how your mind works. You take in information from the environment and you have some choice in that area—that is, in what you take in and what you don't. However, shortly afterward your mind goes on automatic and your thoughts and emotions seem to come and go independently. That's useful in many respects, even though there is a loss of freedom in being automatic. Actually, this loss of freedom creates opportunities for a different kind of freedom. It would be cumbersome if you had to give conscious attention to every detail of life, such as how to understand language, speak, read, walk, and run. It is much more efficient for these abilities to operate largely at an unconscious, automatic level. The same applies to your mental functioning in the area of emotions, feelings, and thoughts. They are often quite automatic. However, through consciousness you have access to freedom. Consciousness is your own personal mirror that helps you to notice what you're doing. With the techniques and concepts covered in this book, you are able to reclaim your freedom whenever you need it and to change the way your mind operates. Of course, after you change your mind—for example, exchanging healthy beliefs for unhealthy ones—it goes on automatic again and preferably in healthy directions. But as long as you exercise consciousness and use these techniques when you need them, mental, emotional, and behavioral freedom will always be available to you.

Skepticism

Initially I was skeptical about energetic approaches, since the idea of treating psychological problems by tapping on your body seemed strange. Possibly this has been your experience too. Anyway, I decided to give tapping a try. First, I treated myself. I used to be afraid of heights and I eliminated this fear with a few minutes of tapping on myself while climbing up a twenty-foot ladder. This technique also worked for social anxiety and a number of personal traumas. I physically tapped on specific acupoints while recalling the memory or being in a situation that caused emotional discomfort. Initially this seemed like simple distraction. However, when the fear of heights and social anxiety did not return, and when the painful memories ceased to be distressing, I immediately disqualified the distraction theory. A better explanation was needed.

An essential feature of the ET approach involves bringing the problem to mind and then stimulating your body in specific ways, such as tapping on acupoints. Although I overcame panic attacks by staying present, observing the panic, and trying to intensify it (see chapter 1), most people who suffer from panic are unable or unwilling to try that approach. But tapping makes it easier to stay present while creating a feeling of calmness and relaxation. Yet the results are not limited to relaxation; you also experience a deep shift in understanding and consciousness. After treating trauma in this way, you often become more philosophical and spiritual about what happened to you. I regularly hear comments like these from people who were previously tormented by trauma: "It doesn't bother me now," "Oh, it's just something that happened a long time ago," "I know that I'm strong. I don't know why it bothered me for so long," "I feel more relaxed now, more at peace. The anger and resentment are gone." I hope you will soon be making similar comments.

How and Why Energy Tapping Works

How can you account for the therapeutic results of stimulating your body in the various ways covered in this book while tuning in a trauma or other psychological problem? What do the techniques really do? These issues were touched on earlier in this book, but now that you have experienced ET it's time to take a closer look.

Placebo Effect

There are many possible explanations as to why ET works. Placebo effect is one suggested mechanism. A placebo is an inert substance or procedure—for example, a capsule that contains sugar rather than a medication. But the "placebo effect" is actual improvement as a result of believing that the substance or procedure will help you. All medications and therapies instill some placebo effect, and there is very little difference between some medications and placebos! But in most cases the magnitude of the placebo effect is no more than 30 percent. That is, generally no more than 30 percent of the positive effects of a medication or procedure are the result of your belief that you will be helped by it. Although you should never underestimate the power of faith and belief, since so many people find that ET and other EP techniques produce highly consistent results, placebo effect has only a little to do with it. Nevertheless, ET probably works best if you also have a fair level of belief in it and in your ability to get better.

Distraction

Another possible explanation is that these techniques are simply distraction. If you are experiencing distress about something, distraction can interrupt the distress. But when you are no longer distracted, the upset can easily return. Of course, being able to distract yourself from distressing thoughts is often very helpful. However, while it is difficult for you to maintain complete focus on the problem while using ET, the distraction theory is insufficient, since the relief continues after you stop using the technique.

Thought Changing

"Cognitive restructuring" is a technique for identifying and altering negative thinking. To do this, you challenge the thoughts so that your negative emotional reaction can be relieved. Related to this is "reframing," which involves a shift in how you think about an issue from negative to positive. Since changes in thought and perception spontaneously occur with these techniques, it may look like cognitive restructuring and reframing are the responsible ingredients. However, with ET the cognitive shifts occur after the negative emotion has been relieved through tapping or other techniques. This is really quite the opposite of what happens with cognitive restructuring. While a positive shift in cognition can serve to support healthy psychological functioning, ET treatments do not directly address cognition as the lever for initial change.

Intention

Some people say that these techniques work because of the user's intention. This seems to be saying that anything will work as long as you have the right intention. I think this is how intention works: If you jump out of an airplane from two thousand feet with a parachute and your intention is to reach the ground safely, you'll pull the ripcord and probably reach the ground safely. However, if you jump out of an airplane from two thousand feet without a parachute and intend to reach the ground safely, you won't. Intention is absolutely important, but it also requires proper action and techniques that can work. ET supports your intention.

Brain Anatomy

Certainly the brain is involved in the changes brought about through these techniques. If you look at the basic formula, it's apparent that the trauma needs to be tuned in if it is going to be effectively treated. This means that you need to think about the trauma, and when you think, you use your brain and other parts of your body. And when you bring a traumatic memory to mind, those areas where trauma is stored get activated. For example, neuroscientists have found that specific areas of the limbic system are involved in trauma, such as the amygdala and hippocampus. So when you attune to the trauma, these areas are "online." Obviously since ET techniques effectively eliminate trauma, they change the way trauma is stored in your brain and your body. Yet since your brain and body operate electrically, energy is also involved.

One aspect of this energy field is the synapse, which is the gap between neurons or brain cells. Electrical impulses travel along the neuron, reach the synapse, and then interact with neurotransmitters (chemicals) that adjust the flow of the electrical impulse. Some of these chemicals decrease the impulse and others intensify it. Whatever you do involves neurons firing. The more frequently a group of neurons fires, the more likely they will fire as a group again. Neurons that fire together wire together. They form an association. This is referred to as Hebb's law. When you have a memory, a network of neurons is firing. When you have a trauma, a network of neurons is firing. Memory, trauma, psychological symptoms, and resilience all involve neurons firing in specific arrangements. When you use ET techniques, the arrangement of neurons firing is changed. For example, tapping while tuning in a trauma causes other neurons to fire and these neurons wire together (Hebb's law) with the neurons that perpetuate the trauma. In the future when the trauma neurons fire, the new neurons previously activated by tapping also fire. This changes the arrangement and your experience. The trauma is gone.

Brain Chemistry

Since acupoints are often stimulated in ET, neurotransmitters and endorphins play a role in the treatment effects—similar to what has been found to be the case with acupuncture. While acupoint stimulation activates the central nervous system to alter brain chemistry, this does not exclude energetic effects. There is a signaling mechanism associated with the acupuncture meridians and nerves leading from the body to the spinal cord and brain that figures into such action. The other techniques covered in this book must also affect brain chemistry and your energy system.

Holistic Effects

The effectiveness of ET involves many dimensions. While your brain, body, neurochemistry, cognition, distraction, intention, and belief, as well as the placebo effect, are involved in the efficacy of ET, energy is also fundamental. After all, everything in our physical reality is basically energy.

Trauma is stored as an energy field, similar to the electromagnetic patterns or information on a computer hard drive, CD, or MP3 player. A traumatic event is like throwing stones into a pond with the trauma being the resulting splashes and ripples. Of course, ponds are highly proficient at getting over trauma quickly, since the splashes and ripples smooth out within a few minutes. Human beings, on the other hand, are adept at capturing and storing trauma. It is as if people are ponds that freeze at the moment of impact and the informational ripples become frozen in time. Your nervous system, cells, and energy system capture and store the trauma.

Trauma begins as a traumatic event that you experience with your senses, your thoughts, and your past history. If your past history was nurturing and protective, the event may have less impact than if your personal history was abusive and neglectful. However, some traumatic events are so horrid and pervasive that even a foundation of security may not protect you from developing trauma.

The experience of the traumatic event is also energetic, since light and sound are forms of energy that stimulate your senses. This input is converted into electrical impulses in your nervous system, body, and energy system. Within your brain, these impulses are converted into chemicals. Then the chemicals stimulate the development of proteins that store the trauma. With trauma, a physical change eventually occurs that begins as energy. Any long-term memory has this basic characteristic. At the same time, the memory of the event involves neurons or brain cells firing in a specific arrangement. In the future, internal and environmental triggers will activate this arrangement of neurons, which includes chemical and energetic activity. The triggers include sight, sound, smell, taste, physical sensations, and even memories and thoughts. It also seems likely that trauma causes genetic changes that in turn maintain the trauma.

Another possibility is that trauma and other psychological problems are contained within a much more pervasive field that is not limited to your nervous system. In addition to the possibility of meridians, chakras, and auras, there is evidence that your cells communicate through light and sound frequencies (Popp and Beloussov 2003;

Benveniste, Aïssa, and Guillonnet 1998). As the light and sound information zooms around inside your physical body, it also travels outward. It seems that you are pulsating with energy and information. And when you have trauma, this entire energy field that you are is involved.

The techniques covered in this book are intended to eliminate the trauma at the energy level. Since energy is the initial domino in the sequence of events that cause the trauma, producing an energetic shift must result in cognitive, chemical, and physical changes as well. Treating trauma in this way is thorough. The trauma is truly gone.

Spreading the Wealth

Now that you've read *Energy Tapping for Trauma*, please continue to use this as a resource manual. The more you use these concepts and techniques, the better it gets, since practice makes perfect. Please share this information with family, friends, acquaintances, and clients so they can also benefit. It's possible that the majority of emotional and behavioral problems have their roots in trauma. As trauma is significantly reduced in our societies, many personal and societal problems will be eliminated. If you share these tools with six people and they in turn share similarly (and on and on), it won't be long before these concepts and techniques become household tools and the mental health of our communities and nations will improve dramatically. That's a contribution worth making.

Appendix A: Acronyms

Acupoints/Tapping Techniques

A—armpit, toward the front

BB—Brain Balancer

BH—back of hand

CH—on the upper chest, upper part of sternum (over the thymus gland)

EB—beginning of eyebrows near bridge of nose

EER—Elaborated Eye Roll

ER—Eye Roll

GT—inside edge of big toenails

IA—upper edge of the inner ankle bones

IF—inside tip of either index fingernail

LF—inside tip of either little fingernail

LT—little toenail

SH—side of hand

SN—side of nostril (either side of nose on the face)

SS—sore spot (a tender spot between the second and third ribs above the breast on the left side of the chest).

TE—third-eye point, between and slightly above the eyebrows

UA—six inches under one or both armpits

UBL—under bottom lip

UCB—under one or both collarbones next to sternum

UE—under one or both eyes on the bony orbit

UK—under knee

UN—under nose

Other Terms

ADHD—attention-deficit/hyperactivity disorder

AEP—Advanced Energy Psychology™

AK—applied kinesiology

ASD—acute stress disorder

BK—behavioral kinesiology

BPS—best possible self

CAPs—complementary and alternative psychotherapies

CBT—cognitive behavioral therapy

CNS—central nervous system

DES—disorders of extreme stress

DID—dissociative identity disorder

ECT—Energy Consciousness Therapy™

ED—energy disorganization

EDxTM—Energy Diagnostic and Treatment Methods™

EFT—emotional freedom techniques

EMDR—eye movement desensitization and reprocessing

EMI—eye movement integration

EP—energy psychology

ESP—Eight-Step Process™

ESR—emotional stress release

ET—energy tapping

EvTFT—evolving thought field therapy

FOH—frontal/occipital holding

HBLU—Healing from the Body Level Up

HELP—Healing Energy Light Process™

HRV—heart-rate variability

ICAK—International College of Applied Kinesiology

LOD—level of discomfort

LOH—level of happiness

MAOI—monoamine oxidase inhibitor

MET—Midline Energy Treatment™

MTBI—mild traumatic brain injury

NAEM—Negative Affect Erasing Method™

PR—psychological reversal

REBT—rational emotive behavior therapy

SNDRI—serotonin, norepinephrine, and dopamine reuptake inhibitor

S-R—stimulus-response

SSNRI—selective serotonin and norepinephrine reuptake inhibitor

SSRI—selective serotonin reuptake inhibitor

SUD—subjective units of discomfort (or distress)

SUG—subjective units of gratitude

SUU—subjective units of upset

TCAs—tricyclic and tetracyclic antidepressants

TFH—touch for health

TFT—thought field therapy

TIR—traumatic incident reduction

TRT—Trauma Removal Technique™

USP—Unified Self Process™

V/KD—visual-kinesthetic dissociation

Appendix B:
Research in Energy Psychology

The first reported research in energy psychology (EP) was a case report from 1980, and since that time the number of reports has grown steadily. Several additional case examples are noted in this book. See the discussions about Barbara, Bill, Amanda, and Carl in chapter 5.

Case Reports

The first case report from Dr. Roger J. Callahan was about Mary, who had a severe water phobia from early childhood (Gallo 2005). Mary had difficulty taking a bath, could not go out of the house when it was raining, and had weekly nightmares about water consuming her. This phobia appeared to be hereditary, since she had it all her life and there was no evidence of a traumatic event. Mary was in treatment for about eighteen months and experienced little progress even after a variety of therapy techniques were tried with her. After a period of cognitive therapy, hypnosis, and behavior therapy, she eventually was able to sit near the shallow end of a swimming pool and dangle her feet in the water. However, she could not look at the water and she would get a severe headache after each session.

Given such little progress, Dr. Callahan decided to try a new approach with her based on applied kinesiology (AK) and acupressure. He asked her to think about water while he gently tapped on the bony orbits under her eyes with his fingertips. Within a minute or so, Mary said that she no longer got a sick feeling in her stomach while thinking about water. She then went outside to the swimming pool, looked at the water, and with delight she vigorously splashed water in her face! Mary's fear of water remained permanently cured after the few minutes of this odd therapy.

Clinical Research

While case studies are interesting and informative, they are not considered to be scientific proof of the effectiveness of a therapeutic approach. It is possible that the success with Mary, Barbara, Bill, and other clients treated with EP was due to factors other than the tapping. For example, since individual cases do not include a placebo control group, the placebo effect is a possible explanation. Placebo effect suggests that the reasons the patients got better was because they believed that EP was going to help them. But why didn't they believe in the other established approaches that were used with them? It's likely that placebo effect would have occurred earlier. The therapists' enthusiasm or the accumulative effects of all the therapy done with these patients might be plausible explanations too. But why would therapists use methods that they didn't feel positive about? I find these and other explanations difficult to accept. Rather, I firmly believe that the tapping while attuning the trauma or other psychological problem made it possible for these patients to get better so quickly.

Nevertheless, from the standpoint of science more is needed before an approach can be considered to be widely effective. Although there have been over a dozen studies on EP, only a few have been published in scientific journals. Several studies have supported the effectiveness of EP in the treatment of phobias and anxiety disorders, including fear of heights (acrophobia), blood-injection-injury phobia, public speaking anxiety, and post-traumatic stress disorder (PTSD), in addition to a variety of other psychological problems.

In 1987, an informal study showed significant decrease in subjective units of discomfort (SUD) of call-in subjects treated with thought field therapy (TFT) on radio talk shows (Callahan 1987). This study was later replicated by Dr. Glen Leonoff, who obtained equivalent results (Leonoff 1996). However, these were not highly scientific studies, since they could not include control groups, placebo treatments, follow-up evaluations, or other measures that are typically included in scientific experiments. Although many researchers would dismiss these studies, since they only showed a decrease in SUD, it is interesting that the same criticism is not raised when a study shows that a tranquilizer relieves anxiety. Most follow-up studies would not support the effectiveness of the tranquilizer in relieving the anxiety after the drug has been discontinued. Nevertheless, the ability of a treatment to give temporary relief is considered acceptable by the medical community and the patient.

These studies each had 68 subjects with various phobias and anxiety problems. All told, 132 of the 136 subjects were successfully treated. This translates into a 97 percent success rate, which is really unheard of in the area of psychological treatment! The average pretreatment SUD rating (on a 10-point scale) was over 8, and after treatment they ranged from 1.50 to 2.10. Further, the treatment times ranged from four to six minutes, which is again unheard of with psychological treatment.

In 1995, researchers at Florida State University conducted a systematic clinical demonstration project that evaluated the effectiveness of TFT and three other brief treatments for trauma and PTSD (Carbonell and Figley 1999). This was more sophisticated and detailed research that included evaluations of the subjects throughout the course of the study. Follow-up evaluations within four to six months showed that all of the approaches were effective in reducing SUD levels. However, EP was the fastest and showed the greatest overall decrease in SUD.

Earlier experimental research looked at the TFT phobia treatment and the effects on self-concept (Wade 1990). Two self-concept questionnaires were used to evaluate subjects with various phobias. Sixteen of the subjects treated with TFT had a drop in SUD ratings of 4 or more points, while only four of the no-treatment controls showed a decrease in SUD of 2 or more points. Two months after treatment, statistical tests revealed significant improvements in the TFT-treated subjects' self-acceptance and self-esteem. Results supported the effectiveness of TFT for the treatment of phobias and for improving self-concept.

Another experiment evaluated the effectiveness of TFT in the treatment of height phobia, or acrophobia (Carbonell 1997). The 49 college students were initially screened from a total of 156 students with an acrophobia questionnaire. All of the students completed a behavioral task, which involved approaching and possibly climbing a four-foot ladder. A four-foot path leading to the ladder was also calibrated in one-foot segments. As the students approached and climbed the ladder, SUD ratings were taken at each floor segment and rung of the ladder. The students were permitted to discontinue the task at any time. After these measures were obtained, each student met with an experimenter in a separate room and a SUD rating was obtained while the student thought about an anxiety-provoking situation related to height. The students were then randomly assigned to one of two groups: TFT phobia treatment or placebo "treatment." All of the students were treated for psychological reversal, whether they had it or not. The placebo group tapped at body areas not used in TFT. After the TFT treatment was done, SUD measures were taken again. If the student did not get a rating of 0, the procedure (treatment or placebo) was administered once again. Although both treatment and control groups showed improvement (maybe because of the treatment for reversal and because body stimulation itself has some therapeutic effects), the TFT students had significantly greater improvement, especially while actually approaching and climbing the ladder.

An additional phobia study involved TFT treatment of twenty subjects with blood-injection-injury phobia (Darby 2001). Measures included SUD and a fear inventory. Treatment time was limited to one hour with the energy diagnostic approach used in TFT. Although this study contains many methodological flaws, one-month follow-up measures yielded statistically significant treatment effects.

A trauma case study used the TFT diagnostic approach combined with a measure of brain waves, or electroencephalogram (qEEG), to assess physiological changes after treatment (Diepold and Goldstein 2000). Statistically abnormal brain-wave patterns were recorded when the patient thought about a trauma compared to a neutral (baseline) event. Reassessment of the brain-wave patterns associated with the traumatic memory immediately after TFT revealed no statistical abnormalities. Eighteen months later a reevaluation showed that the patient continued to be free of emotional upset regarding the treated trauma and the brain-wave pattern remained normal.

During five separate two-week trips in the year 2000, therapists reported on uncontrolled treatment of trauma victims in Kosovo with TFT (Johnson et al. 2001). Treatments were given to 105 Albanian patients with 249 separate violent traumatic incidents. The traumas included rape, torture, and witnessing the massacre of loved ones. Total relief of the traumas was reported by 103 of the patients and for 247 of the 249 separate traumas treated. Follow-up data averaging five months revealed no relapses. While this data is based on uncontrolled treatments, the absence of relapse ought to arouse attention, since a 98 percent spontaneous remission of PTSD is unlikely.

To provide a measure of the scope of EP, another study demonstrated clinical and statistical significance of TFT used with 714 patients who suffered from a variety of psychological problems. The patients' conditions included anxiety, adjustment disorder with anxiety and depression, anxiety due to medical condition, anger, acute stress, bereavement, chronic pain, cravings, panic, PTSD, trichotillomania (hair pulling), and more (Sakai et al. 2001).

An additional study involved thirty-nine uncontrolled cases that were treated for a variety of clinical problems with TFT, observing that in most cases improvement in SUD coincided with improvement in heart-rate variability (HRV). HRV is a measure of the health of the heart, and it is not easily affected by conscious choice and tends to be stable and placebo free (Pignotti and Steinberg 2001).

Several EP approaches have been subjected to experimental tests. A recent trial compared diaphragmatic breathing with *emotional freedom techniques* (EFT), which involved tapping on several meridian acupoints for the treatment of specific phobias of small animals (Wells et al. 2003). Subjects were randomly assigned and treated individually for thirty minutes with either EFT (eighteen subjects) or diaphragmatic breathing (seventeen subjects). Statistical analyses revealed that both treatments produced significant improvements in phobic reactions, although tapping on meridian points produced significantly greater improvement behaviorally and on three self-report measures. The greater improvement for the energy technique was maintained at six to nine months follow-up on avoidance behavior. These results were achieved in a single thirty-minute treatment without inducing the anxiety typical of traditional exposure therapies and without live exposure to the animals during the treatment phases. Since similar levels of imaginary exposure, experimental demand, and cognitive processing were present in the two treatment conditions, this suggests that additional factors contributed to the results achieved by the EP treatment. The researchers suggested that intervening in the body's energy system through the meridian acupoints may have been the deciding factor. These results are certainly encouraging about the effectiveness of meridian-based therapies with specific phobias.

Another EFT study focused on subjects who had been involved in motor vehicle accidents and who experienced post-traumatic stress associated with the accident (Swingle, Pulos, and Swingle 2005). All subjects received two treatment sessions and all reported improvement immediately following treatment. Brain-wave assessments before and after treatment indicated that subjects who maintained the benefit of the treatments showed unique brain-wave patterns. This study also indicated that the treatment effects of EP involve positive neurologic changes.

A somewhat perplexing study examined EFT for phobias and other fears with a sample of 119 nonclinical university students who were treated in group settings (Waite and Holder 2003). The four treatment conditions included EFT, placebo control (tapping sham points on the arms), modeling (tapping the EFT points on a doll), and no-treatment controls. A statistically significant decrease in SUD occurred with all three treatment groups. Interestingly, tapping at locations other than the EFT points as well as tapping at EFT acupoints on the doll had the greatest improvement! Although this was not a patient population, the study suggests that treatment effects can be achieved through simply stimulating your body and vicariously through observing tapping.

Another EFT study involved 102 participants who were rated on a symptom checklist one month before and at the beginning of an EFT workshop (Rowe 2005). The subjects were also tested at the conclusion of the workshop in addition to follow-ups at one month and six months. There was a statistically significant decrease in all measures of psychological distress during all follow-up assessments.

A doctoral dissertation experimental study of the EP technique Be Set Free Fast (BSFF), which involves a four-point tapping routine combined with affirmations, suggests that this approach is effective in the treatment of insect phobia (Christoff 2003). This research involved four single case studies. Two of the subjects were phobic of crickets, one of ants, and one of caterpillars and worms. For each subject, extensive pre- and post-testing was done during six twice-weekly sessions to establish baselines, followed by six treatment sessions and evaluation. Continued monitoring with psychological instruments was conducted at the six treatment sessions. Also SUD and heart-rate measures were obtained throughout the study. The major portion of phobic reduction occurred during the first treatment session, with some additional improvement in the next two sessions. All clients experienced significant drops in their phobic symptoms and were no longer having anxiety in the presence of the phobic object.

A pilot study examined the effects of energy psychology on claustrophobia with four claustrophobic subjects and four normal controls (Lambrou, Pratt, and Chevalier 1999). All subjects were evaluated with pencil-paper tests, biofeedback measures, and SUD and behavioral measures before and after treatment and at an approximately two-week follow-up. A unique feature of this study is that the electrical properties in the acupuncture system were measured. Statistical analysis revealed significant differences before and after treatment between the control group and the claustrophobic group. The researchers noted that the measures of autonomic functions included in the study are less susceptible to placebo or positive expectancy effects.

The most extensive preliminary clinical study on the effectiveness of energy psychology was conducted in South America over fourteen years with 31,400 patients (Andrade and Feinstein 2004). A substudy of this group took place over five and a half years with 5,000 patients diagnosed with PTSD and other psychological disorders. Included in the substudy were only those conditions in which energy psychology and a standard of care control group (cognitive behavioral therapy [CBT] plus medication when indicated) could be used. At the end of treatment and at follow-up periods of one month, three months, six months, and twelve months, the patients were interviewed by telephone by interviewers that had not been involved in the patients' treatment. These follow-up interviews revealed a 90 percent positive clinical response and a 76 percent complete elimination of symptoms with energy psychology alone. There was a 63 percent positive response and a 51 percent complete elimination of symptoms with CBT/medication. These results are exceptionally significant, suggesting that energy psychology was superior to CBT/medication for a wide range of psychological disorders. Furthermore, the average number of sessions in the CBT/medication group was fifteen, while the average number of sessions in the energy psychology group was only three.

There are a number of EP studies that were not completed or published at the time of this review. Within the next few years, many more studies will appear in journals and other publications. It is highly probable that an increasing number of studies will support the effectiveness of EP approaches and decipher the most essential elements in this new and exciting therapeutic approach.

Appendix C: Resources

Books and Manuals

Diepold, John, Victoria Britt, and Sheila Bender. 2004. *Evolving Thought Field Therapy.* New York: Norton.

Feinstein, David. 2004. *Energy Psychology Interactive.* Ashland, OR: Innersource.

Furman, Mark, and Fred P. Gallo. 2000. *The Neurophysics of Human Behavior: Explorations at the Interface of Brain, Mind, Behavior, and Information.* Boca Raton, FL: CRC Press.

Gallo, Fred. 2000. *Energy Diagnostic and Treatment Methods.* New York: Norton.

———, ed. 2002. *Energy Psychology in Psychotherapy: A Comprehensive Source Book.* New York: Norton.

Gallo, Fred. 2005 *Energy Psychology: Explorations at the Interface of Energy, Cognition, Behavior, and Health (second edition).* Boca Raton: CRC Press.

Gallo, Fred, and Harry Vincenzi. 2000. *Energy Tapping: How to Rapidly Eliminate Anxiety, Depression, Cravings, and More Using Energy Psychology.* Oakland, CA: New Harbinger Publications.

Hartung, John, and Michael Galvin. 2003. *Energy Psychology and EMDR: Combining Forces to Optimize Treatment.* New York: Norton.

Hover-Kramer, Dorothea. 2002. *Creative Energies: Psychotherapy for Self-Expression and Healing.* New York: Norton.

CDs, Audiotapes, and DVDs

Feinstein, David. 2004. *Energy Psychology Interactive* [CD]. This excellent program teaches energy psychology basics and even some advanced protocols. A great professional complement to this book, the CD covers many aspects of energy psychology in an interactive format.
Published by and available from Innersource, Ashland, OR
www.innersource.net

Gallo, Fred P. 2007. *Energy Tapping for Trauma* [DVD]. This DVD illustrates many of the techniques covered in this book, *Energy Tapping for Trauma.* Dr. Gallo provides discussion and commentary, and guides you and a client through the techniques.
(724) 346-3838
www.energypsych.com

Gallo, Fred P. 2007. *Healing Energy Light Process* (HELP)™ [CD]. This CD offers several versions of HELP, one of which is covered in *Energy Tapping for Trauma.* The voice of Dr. Gallo guides you through this healing journey.
(724) 346-3838
www.energypsych.com

Gallo, Fred, and Mary Wheeler. 2002. *Healing Energy Light Process* (HELP)™ [Audiotape]. The soothing voice of Dr. Mary S. Wheeler guides you through the original version of HELP.
(724) 346-3838
www.energypsych.com

E-mail Discussion Groups

EnerGym Email List (moderated by Dr. Fred Gallo). To subscribe, send an e-mail to:
energym-subscribe@yahoogroups.com

Energyspirit1 e-mail discussion list (moderated by Dr. Phil Friedman). To subscribe, send an e-mail to:
PhilF101@aol.com

Institute for Meridian Psychotherapy and Counseling list. To subscribe, send a blank e-mail to:
IMPC.Forum-subscribe@listbot.com

Energy Psychology Therapists, Information, and Training

Association for Comprehensive Energy Psychology (ACEP): Provides annual conferences, support to the field of energy psychology, and lists of EP practitioners.
www.energypsych.org

Dr. Gallo's Energy Psychology home page: Covers free information on energy psychology; training in Advanced Energy Psychology (AEP)™, Energy Diagnostic and Treatment Methods (EDxTM)™, and Energy Consciousness Therapy (ECT)™; certified AEP practitioners and trainers; and more.
www.energypsych.com

Other Resources

Several of these sources also provide information on contacting qualified EP practitioners.

Acupower
www.freedomfromfearforever.com

BE SET FREE FAST
www.BeSetFreeFast.com

Callahan Techniques/TFT
www.tftrx.com

Emotional Freedom Techniques
www.emofree.com

Evolving Thought Field Therapy (EvTFT)
www.tftworldwide.com

Healing from the Body Level Up (HBLU)
www.jaswack.com

Seemorg Matrix Work
www.seemorgmatrix.org

Tapas Acupressure Technique
www.tatlife.com

Related Training and Information

Colorado Consulting Group
DrGalvin@earthlink.net

David Baldwin's Trauma Information Pages
www.trauma-pages.com

EMDR International Association (EMDRIA)
www.emdria.org

PsychInnovations
www.psychinnovations.com/y1inner.htm

Energy Psychology Training Locations

Austria

Institut Dr. Schmida, Vienna
institut@schmida.com
www.schmida.com

Institut für Kind, Jugend und Familie, Graz
ikjf@utanet.at
www.ikjf.at

Canada

Lesley Hannell Corvino, MA, Hamilton (Dundas), Ontario
lesley@hannellcorvino.com
www.hannellcorvino.com

Georgian Bay NLP Centre, Toronto, Ontario
gbnlp@gb-nlp.com
www.gb-nlp.com

Meridian Seminars, Toronto, Ontario
www.TorontoEPC.com

Germany

Institut für Angewandte Kinesiologie (IAK GmbH), Kirchzarten bei Freiburg
info@iak-freiburg.de
www.iak-freiburg.de

Institut für Coaching, Bildung, und Gesundheit, Hamburg
institut@dr-karin-hauffe.de
www.coaching-und-bildung.de

Milton Erickson Institut Berlin
mail@erickson-institut-berlin.de
www.erickson-institut-berlin.de

Milton-Erickson-Institut Heidelberg
office@meihei.de
www.meihei.de

Privatklinik Bad Zwischenahn, Bad Zwischenahn
www.privatklinik-zwischenahn.de
www.dagmar-ingwersen.de

Switzerland

Praxis für systemische Energiebalance, Jonen
aurelia.reist@familiensystem.ch
www.familiensystem.ch

United Kingdom

The Association for Meridian Energy Therapies (AMT)
Eastbourne, East Sussex, UK
Theamt.com

USA

Anthony Robbins Companies, San Diego, CA
www.anthonyrobbinsdc.com

National Institute for the Clinical Application of Behavioral Medicine
(NICABM), Mansfield Center, CT
information@nicabm.com
www.nicabm.com

Southeast Institute for Group and Family Therapy, Chapel Hill, NC
vjoines@seinstitute.com
www.seinstitute.com

References

American Psychiatric Association. 2000. *Diagnostic and Statistical Manual of Mental Disorders*. 4th ed., text revision. Washington, DC: American Psychiatric Association.

Andrade, J., and D. Feinstein. 2004. Energy psychology: Theory, indications, evidence. In D. Feinstein, *Energy Psychology Interactive* [CD]. Ashland, OR: Innersource.

Andreas, S., and C. Andreas. 1995. *Eye Movement Integration (applied with a Vietnam Veteran who has been experiencing intrusive memories)*. Videotape. Boulder, CO: NLP Comprehensive.

Bandler, R., and J. Grinder. 1979. *Frogs into Princes*. Moab, UT: Real People Press.

Benveniste, J., J. Aïssa, and D. Guillonnet. 1998. Digital biology: Specificity of the digitized molecular signal. *FASEB Journal* 12:A412.

Boudewyns, P. A., and L. Hyer. 1990. Physiological response to combat memories and preliminary treatment outcome in Vietnam veteran PTSD patients treated with direct therapeutic exposure. *Behavior Therapy* 21:63–87.

Brom, D., R. J. Klebar, and P. B. Defares. 1989. Brief psychotherapy for posttraumatic stress disorders. *Journal of Consulting and Clinical Psychology* 57:607–12.

Burr, H. S. 1972. *Blueprint for Immortality: The Electric Patterns of Life*. Essex, England: Saffron Walden.

Callahan, R. J. 1985. *Five Minute Phobia Cure*. Wilmington, DE: Enterprise.

———. 1987. Successful treatment of phobias and anxiety by telephone and radio. Collected Papers of *International College of Applied Kinesiology* (Shawnee Mission, KS), Winter: 7–15.

Carbonell, J. 1997. An experimental study of TFT and acrophobia. *The Thought Field* 2(3):1–6.

Carbonell, J. L., and C. R. Figley. 1999. A systematic clinical demonstration project of promising PTSD treatment approaches. *Traumatology* 5(1):32–48.

Childre, D., and H. Martin (with D. Beech). 1999. *The HeartMath Solution*. San Francisco: HarperCollins.

Christoff, K. M. 2003. Treating specific phobias with BE SET FREE FAST: A meridian based sensory intervention. Ph.D. diss., Trinity College of Graduate Studies (Anaheim, CA).

Coccaro, E. F., J. L. Siever, H. M. Klar, G. Maurer, K. Cochrane, T. B. Cooper, R. C. Mohs, and K. L. Davis. 1989. Serotonergic studies in patients with affective and personality disorders: Correlates with suicidal and impulsive aggressive behavior. *Archives of General Psychiatry* 46:587–99.

Cook, A., and R. Bradshaw. 1999. *Toward Integration: One Eye at a Time*. Vancouver, BC: One-Eye Press.

Cooper, N. A., and G. A. Clum. 1989. Imaginal flooding as a supplementary treatment for PTSD in combat veterans: A controlled study. *Behavior Therapy* 20:381–91.

Darby, D. 2001. The efficiency of thought field therapy as a treatment modality for individuals diagnosed with blood-injection-injury phobia. Ph.D. diss., Walden University (Minneapolis, MN).

de Jong, J., T. V. M. Komproe, H. Ivan, M. von Ommeren, M. El Masri, M. Araya, N. Khaled, W. van de Put, and D. J. Somasundarem. 2001. Lifetime events and posttraumatic stress disorder in 4 postconflict settings. *Journal of the American Medical Association* 286(5):555–62.

Depue, R. A., and M. R. Spoont. 1986. Conceptualizing a serotonin trait: A behavioral dimension of constraint. *Annals of the New York Academy of Sciences* 487:47–62.

de Vernejoul, P., P. Albarede, and J. C. Darras. 1985. Etude des meridiens d'acupuncture par les traceurs radioactifs. [Study of the acupuncture meridians with radioactive tracers.] *Bulletin of the Academy of National Medicine* (Paris) 169:1071–75.

Diamond, J. 1985. *Life Energy*. New York: Dodd, Mead and Company.

Diepold, J. H., Jr., and D. Goldstein. 2000. Thought field therapy and qEEG changes in the treatment of trauma: A case study. Moorestown, NJ: Author.

Emmons, R. A., and M. E. McCullough. 2003. Counting blessings versus burdens: Experimental studies of gratitude and subjective well-being in daily life. *Journal of Personality and Social Psychology* 84:377–89.

———. 2004. *The Psychology of Gratitude.* New York: Columbia University Press.

Foa, E. B., R. O. Rothbaum, D. Riggs, and T. Murdock. 1991. Treatment of post-traumatic stress disorder in rape victims: A comparison between cognitive-behavioral procedures and counseling. *Journal of Consulting and Clinical Psychology* 59:715–23.

Frankl, V. 1959. *Man's Search for Meaning: An Introduction to Logotherapy.* New York: Washington Square Press.

Gallo, F. P. 2000. *Energy Diagnostic and Treatment Methods.* New York: Norton.

———, ed. 2002. *Energy Psychology in Psychotherapy: A Comprehensive Source Book.* New York: Norton.

———. 2005. *Energy Psychology: Explorations at the Interface of Energy, Cognition, Behavior, and Health.* Boca Raton, FL: CRC Press.

Gallo, F. P., and H. Vincenzi. 2000. *Energy Tapping: How to Rapidly Eliminate Anxiety, Depression, Cravings, and More Using Energy Psychology.* Oakland, CA: New Harbinger Publications.

Gerbode, F. 1989. *Beyond Psychology: An Introduction to Metapsychology.* Palo Alto, CA: IRM Press.

Herman, J. 1992. *Trauma and Recovery: The Aftermath of Violence—from Domestic Abuse to Political Terror.* New York: Basic Books.

Jenike, M. A., and S. L. Rauch. 1994. Managing the patient with treatment-resistant obsessive-compulsive disorder. *Journal of Clinical Psychiatry* 55 (3):11–17.

Johnson, C., M. Shala, X. Sejdijaj, R. Odell, and K. Dabishevci. 2001. Thought field therapy—soothing the bad moments of Kosovo. *Journal of Clinical Psychology* 57(10):1237–40.

Johnson, R. (with J. Bennette). 1994. *Rapid Eye Technology.* Salem, OR: RainTree Press.

Keane, T. M., J. A. Fairbank, J. M. Caddell, and R. T. Zimmering. 1989. Implosive (flooding) therapy reduces symptoms of PTSD in Vietnam combat veterans. *Behavior Therapy* 20:245–60.

Kelly, G. A. 1955. *The Psychology of Personal Constructs.* New York: Norton.

Kessler, R. C., W. T. Chiu, O. Demler, and E. E. Walters. 2005. Prevalence, severity, and comorbidity of twelve-month DSM-IV disorders in the National Comorbidity Survey Replication (NCS-R). *Archives of General Psychiatry* 62(6):617–27.

Kulka, R. A., W. E. Schlenger, J. A. Fairbank, R. L. Hough, B. K. Jordan, C. R. Marmar, and D. S. Weiss. 1988. Contractual report of findings from the National Vietnam Veterans Readjustment Study. Research Triangle Park, NC: Research Triangle Institute.

Lambrou, P. T., G. T. Pratt, and G. Chevalier. 2003. Physiological and psychological effects of a mind/body therapy on claustrophobia. *Subtle Energies & Energy Medicine* 14(3):239–51.

LeDoux, J. 2002. *Synaptic Self: How Our Brains Become Who We Are.* New York: Penguin.

Leonoff, G. 1996. The successful treatment of phobias and anxiety by telephone and radio: A replication of Callahan's 1987 study. *TFT Newsletter* 1(2):3–4.

Levin, P. A. 1997. *Waking the Tiger: Healing Trauma.* Berkeley, CA: North Atlantic Books.

McClelland, D., and C. Kirshnit. 1988. The effects of motivational arousal through films on salivary immunoglobulin A. *Psychological Health* 2(2):31–52.

Pignotti, M., and M. Steinberg. 2001. Heart rate variability as an outcome measure for thought field therapy in clinical practice. *Journal of Clinical Psychology* 57(10):1193–1206.

Pitman, R. K., B. Altman, E. Greenwald, R. E. Longpre, M. L. Macklin, R. E. Poire, and G. S. Steketee. 1991. Psychiatric complications during flooding therapy for posttraumatic stress disorder. *Journal of Clinical Psychiatry* 52:17–20.

Popp, F. A., and L. Beloussov. 2003. *Integrative Biophysics: Biophotonics.* Dordrecht, The Netherlands: Kluwer Academic Publishers.

Reichmanis, M., A. Marino, and R. Becker. 1975. Electrical correlates of acupuncture. *IEEE Trans Bio-Medical Engineering* 22:533–35.

Rein, G., M. Atkinson, and R. McCraty. 1995. The physiological and psychological effects of compassion and anger. *Journal of Advancement in Medicine* 8(2):87–105.

Rowe, J. E. 2005. The effects of EFT on long-term psychological symptoms. *Counseling and Clinical Psychology Journal* 2(3):104–11.

Sakai, C., D. Paperny, M. Mathews, G. Tanida, G. Boyd, A. Simons, C. Yamamoto, C. Mau, and L. Nutter. 2001. Thought field therapy clinical application: Utilization in an HMO in behavioral medicine and behavioral health services. *Journal of Clinical Psychology* 57:1215–27.

Shapiro, F. 1995. *Eye Movement Desensitization and Reprocessing: Basic Principles, Protocols, and Procedures.* New York: Guilford Press.

Sheldon, K. M., and S. Lyubomirsky. 2006. How to increase and sustain positive emotion: The effects of expressing gratitude and visualizing best possible selves. *Journal of Positive Psychology* 1:73–82.

Swingle, P., L. Pulos, and M. Swingle. 2005. Neurophysiological indicators of EFT treatment of post-traumatic stress. *Subtle Energies & Energy Medicine* 15(1): 75–86.

van der Kolk, B. A., and O. van der Hart. 1991. The intrusive past: The flexibility of memory and the engraving of trauma. *American Imago* 48(4):425–54.

Wade, J. F. 1990. The effects of the Callahan phobia treatment techniques on self concept. Ph.D. diss., The Professional School of Psychological Studies (San Diego, CA):

Waite, W. L., and M. D. Holder. 2003. Assessment of the emotional freedom technique: An alternative treatment for fear. *Scientific Review of Mental Health Practice* 2(1):20–26.

Wells, S., K. Polglase, H. Andrews, P. Carrington, and A. H. Baker. 2003. Evaluation of a meridian-based intervention, emotional freedom techniques (EFT), for reducing specific phobias of small animals. *Journal of Clinical Psychology* 59(9):943–66.

Wolpe, J. 1958. *Psychotherapy by Reciprocal Inhibition.* Stanford, CA: Stanford University Press.

———. 1961. The systematic desensitization treatment of neuroses. *Journal of Nervous and Mental Disorders* 132:189–203.

Fred P. Gallo, Ph.D., clinical psychologist and a pioneer in the field of Energy Psychology, coined the terms "energy psychology" and "energy tapping." He has published numerous articles, chapters, and seven books, including *Energy Tapping, Energy Psychology, and Energy Psychology in Psychotherapy.* The founder of two therapy approaches—Advanced Energy Psychology (AEP)™ and Energy Consciousness Therapy (ECT)™, he maintains a clinical practice in Hermitage, PA, and teaches his methods throughout the United States, Canada, and Europe.

Foreword writer **Anthony Robbins** is author of *Awakening the Giant Within* and father of life coaching.

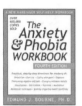

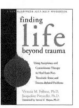